Voices from
the Dressing Floors

Kenidjack Tin Streams c. 1920
Courtesy of Trevithick Society

Voices from the Dressing Floors

1773-1950

First Hand Stories from the Cornish Mines and Quarries

compiled and edited by

Lynne Mayers

Blaize Bailey Books
2009

Back cover illustrations (L to R)

Top row: Peacock Copper (unknown source), Chalcopyrite (Wheal
              Jane), Galena (West Chiverton)

Bottom row: Cassiterite (South Crofty), Wolfram (Cligga Head),
              Malachite (Co. Kerry)

Contents

List of Illustrations

Preface

Over many years, mining engineers and contemporary commentators almost overlooked the importance of describing what it was like to work at the mine or quarry surface, which to them was common-place. Those who developed new dressing techniques sometimes wrote about their success. Well-heeled visitors described their adventures underground. Mining professionals drew beautiful diagrams and described mining machinery minutely. Very rarely have we been left with descriptions of exactly how, or under what conditions, surface workers laboured.

At the other end of the social scale, many of those who worked at surface (certainly, until about 1880) could hardly read or write. Neither would they have the raw material with which to write, nor, more importantly, the time or inclination to record what they would probably prefer to forget.

So who was to write about the everyday, repetitive tasks at surface, which turned rough ore-bearing rock into a valuable commodity? Who was to describe the fine-honed skill of splitting slates? Thankfully, these experiences were recorded by the few, leaving us with precious insights into the world of the stamps, buddle and dressing-horse.

Few they certainly were! Only a handful of real first hand accounts survive. Transcribed, here, are the actual writings of John Harris (poet) of when he worked on Dolcoath dressing floors; of Billy Bray (preacher) when he worked as Surface Captain; of Captain John Jenkin, who worked up through the ranks at Delabole Slate Quarry; and of Richard Lawry and Phyllis Taylor, who worked at Geevor washing floors in the Second World War. Also included are transcriptions of interviews with those who worked at surface: centenarian Susan Robins and Minnie Andrews (the 'last bal maiden'); six Troon women who had worked at mines in their youth; forty young people and four surface captains interviewed in 1841 for the Royal Commission; and six of the women who had worked at Polpuff Glass Mine during the First World War. The story of bal maiden Patty Tremelling is included in full. Although published as an autobiography, it was written posthumously from her journal. We read the words of Samuel Drew through the biography written by his son, and an elderly bal maiden at Carn Brea speaks to us through the records of an American journalist.

The importance of these records should not be underestimated, not just because they are scarce, but because surface workers were the unsung heroes of the mining industry. It was at surface that many famous mine managers or engineers cut their teeth. No-one went underground to work before first having this informal apprenticeship on the dressing floor. Here dressers learnt physics, chemistry, geology, crystallography, economics, and engineering, not from text books but from practical application. They learnt to identify and separate a whole multiplicity of ore types, and the rocks in which they were found. They learnt best angles of cleavage. They learnt about relative densities and how the ores sedimented out differentially on a slope in the racks, strips and buddles, or in layers in the jiggers, pits, and kieves. They learnt the difference between pure, mixed and poor grades of ore. They learnt ergonomics the hard way, in order to wield hammers, carry barrows or shake sieves without causing themselves (or others) injury. They also learnt, through lay-offs and dismissals, what happens when the world price for minerals falls and their labour becomes more expensive than the product they were dressing. In all of this, it was not only the Surface Captain who had to make sound judgements. These surface labourers (male or female, young or old) may not have been book 'learned' but along with stamina and strength they too needed powers of observation, deduction and skill.

The *Voices from the Dressing Floors* that speak to us from the pages of this book do so, on behalf of the many thousands whose voices we cannot hear, and whose stories are lost. These few certainly remind us of the struggle and the cost, for the many. However, more importantly, they also remind us of their achievements, and of their vital contribution to the mineral economy of their day.

Acknowledgements

My thanks go to all those who have contributed to the production of this book; to Mrs. E. Brooke, Cornish Federation of Women's Institutes, Richard Lawry, John Tonkin, and the Cornwall & Devon Media Ltd. for permission to reproduce published or privately-written work; to Tony Brooks and Derek Giles for advice; to the Billy Bray Memorial Trust, Angela Broome (Royal Institution of Cornwall), Stephen Gilbert (Wheal Martyn Archives), Valerie Jacob, Pete Joseph (Trevithick Society), David Thomas (CRO), Neil Williams (Redruth Studies Library), and Geoff Olds (Torquay Museum) for assistance with illustrations; to Catherine Lorigan, Peter Tremewan, Marion Walker and Colin Woolcock for help with research, and to Ian and Peter Boorman for technical assistance. We have attempted to ensure that all copyright acknowledgements are correct, and apologise for any error or oversight.

Chapter 1

Philosophers and Poets in the Making: Samuel Drew and John Harris

From time to time, people emerge from lowly hearths and unpromising situations, not only with brilliant minds, but also with amazing resilience and determination. They are able to fight the social and physical restrictions of poverty and manual labour, and go on to achieve in the academic or artistic world in a most remarkable way. Two such people were Samuel Drew and John Harris.

Both were born to impoverished mining families; Samuel near St. Austell in 1765, and John in the Camborne area, in 1820. Both received only the most basic of formal education, and were largely self-taught. Similarly, both were to begin their working lives on the dressing floors of Cornwall's tin streams or mines and these experiences would colour their attitudes, values and work for the rest of their lives. Both were to publish many books, and both were to be acknowledged as giants in their respective fields of learning; Samuel as a theologian and philosopher, and John as a poet.

Samuel Drew (1765-1833)

Samuel was born at Tregrehan Mill, near St Austell, into a Methodist mining family. After a meagre education, he began work at the age of eight as a buddle boy at the local tin stamps. (Fig. 2 shows tin stamps operating in about 1903, not far from where Samuel must have worked). He remained working at surface for over two years, before being sent as apprentice to a shoemaker.

Samuel began to study seriously during these years of apprenticeship, reading the books that customers brought in for binding. As a young man, he very interested in astronomy and metaphysics, but was happy to read about any subject. By 1787, he had completed his training and set up his own shoemaking business. In the same year he married Honour Halls and, then, became a local preacher. His earliest surviving publication is called *Reflections on St Austell Churchyard 17th August 1792*. This piece includes an elegy to his elder brother, Jabez, on his untimely death. Samuel's son describes how, in these early years, his father studied and wrote 'in a low nursing chair beside the kitchen fire, with bellows as a writing desk, and domestic matters proceeding around him'. As he became well-known, he was nicknamed the *'Metaphysical Shoemaker'*.

Samuel's first major publication *'An Essay on the Immateriality and Immortality of the Human Soul'* was published in 1802. It was so popular that it was also printed in America, and ran to many editions in this country. From 1804 he revised and transcribed the notes which Rev. Thomas Coke had made on his missionary work in the West Indies. Samuel continued this work until Coke's death in 1814. From 1815 until 1824, Samuel continued the compilation of *The History of Cornwall* (a work which had been begun by the late Fortescue Hitchens).

In 1818, Samuel and his family moved from Cornwall to Liverpool, where he was to edit *'The Imperial Magazine or Compendium of Religious, Moral and Philosophical Knowledge'* for Caxton Press, the first edition of which appeared in March 1819. He was soon well known and respected in Liverpool social circles. He was also thought a little eccentric, as suggested by this rhyme which was written about him:

'Long was the man and long was the hair
And long was the coat this long man did wear.'

In 1821, the Caxton Printing Works suffered a catastrophic fire, when all the printing plates and papers were lost. The business was relocated to London, and the Drew family followed. Despite the fact that he was almost entirely self-taught, the Marischal College (Aberdeen) conferred the degree of Artium Magister on Samuel in 1824. He continued writing and editing the *Imperial Magazine* until just a month before his death. Being unwell, he made a long and difficult journey back to Cornwall. Samuel died at Helston, on 29th March 1833, and is buried in Helston Churchyard. He is regarded as Cornwall's *'First Methodist Historian'*. ♪

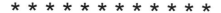

Samuel's eldest son (also Samuel) wrote his biography entitled *Samuel Drew, the Self-Taught Cornishman*, which was published in 1861. In this, he draws on his own memory, on stories told him by his father, and on the recollections of his aunt (his father's only surviving sibling). Reproduced here are those early portions which relate to Samuel's upbringing in this mining household, and his experience as a buddle boy.

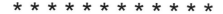

Samuel Drew, the Self-Taught Cornishman
by his eldest son[1]

'In a solitary cottage in the parish of St. Austell, and rather more than a mile eastward from the town, resided a pious couple....their dwelling was very mean, containing a single ground-room, and two bedrooms; and at one end of it was a mill, used to pulverize ore. About half an acre of enclosed ground belonged to the cottage, with which, and the pasturage of the adjoining common, they managed to keep a cow. In this residence they had four children. Samuel, their second son, whose life we record, was born on the third of March, 1765, and baptised in the parish church, on the twenty-fourth of the same month. Jabez, the eldest, who was two years Samuel's senior, died at the age of twenty two; the third child in infancy. To the recollections of Thomasin, the youngest, who outlived her brothers, we are indebted for many of the incidents in Mr. Drew's early life.

At this period, the father's occupation fluctuated between that of husbandman, and what, in Cornwall and Devonshire, is called "streaming for tin": that is, searching the soil and subsoil, examining the deposits of

---

[1] Extracts taken from pp. 17-35

mountain streams, and selecting, by the process of washing and pulverising, such parts as are valuable. By diligence and care, he was enabled to lay by a little money; and soon after the birth of his youngest child, he took a better house, with two or three fields, a short distance from his old habitation. Here, with his scanty capital, he procured a cart and horses, and with them found employment as a carrier.

Notwithstanding their poverty, the parents made every effort to give their children a little education; and for a while, the two boys were sent daily to St. Austell to school. But for Samuel, book learning had no charms…[and he related] *"When I was about six years old, I felt much interested in the different parts of the process of mining, and was very ambitious of sinking a shaft. I prevailed on my brother and another boy to join me, and we commenced operations somewhere near our house. I, though the youngest, was captain; and having procured a board and rope, with pick and a shovel, one drew up with the rope what the others had dug out. We must have followed our task for a considerable time, and sunk our shaft several feet, when my father put an end to our mining operations. A handful of earth being thrown into the pit while I was at work…supposing it to be one of my comrades, I ordered him to desist, and on its being repeated, I, in virtue of my office of captain, threatened him with correction. To my great mortification, my father then appeared…and as a punishment for our clandestine proceeding, assigned us the task of filling it in again."*

Rather more than a year before the mother's death, the parents found it necessary to take their boys from school, by manual labour, that they might assist in their own maintenance. Jabez helped his father in their little farm, and Samuel was employed at a neighbouring stamping-mill, probably attached to the house where he first drew breath.

The mineral, as found below the surface is usually combined with other substances of no value; the proportion of refuse far exceeding that of the ore. The stony mass in which it is commonly lodged, when broken by hammers to a convenient size, is submitted to the action of the stamping-mill, where it is pulverised. This machine is of very simple construction. Heavy iron weights, termed stamp-heads, are attached to perpendicular beams of wood, which are kept in their position by a strong frame. These beams are lifted successively by the revolution of a water-wheel; and by their weight, and the momentum of their fall, the substance is reduced to powder. The pulverised material is then carried by a small stream of water into shallow pits prepared for its reception, where the gravity of the mineral causes it to sink, while the sandy particles pass off with the stream. As this does not produce a sufficient separation, children are employed to stir up the deposit in the pits, and keep it in agitation, until this part of the cleansing process is complete. These pits are called the *buddles*; and they give name to the occupation of the children who labour at them.

At the tender age of eight, Samuel Drew began to work as a *buddle-boy*. For his services, his father was to receive three-half-pence a day; but when the wages of eight weeks had accumulated in the hands of the employer, he became insolvent, and the poor boy's earnings were lost. The mill being now occupied by another person, the wages were raised to two-pence a day, the highest sum Samuel realized in that employment, though he continued to work at it for more than two years.

Fig. 2 Tin stamps at 4 The Court, Tregrehan Mills 1902-03
courtesy of Valerie Jacob née Mugford, St Austell, Cornwall

"I well remember," he once said, *"how much I and the other boys were elated at this advance of wages. Not that we were personally benefited, as our friends[2] received the money; but it added, in thought, to our importance.*

One of my companions, very little older than myself, lived with an aunt, who, on the death of his parents, had kindly brought him up. The additional halfpenny a day so elevated him in his own opinion, that he very gravely went home, and gave his aunt notice, that, as soon as his

---

[2] Probably means relative

wages became due, he should seek new lodgings, and board himself. By the timely application of the rod, she convinced him that the season of independence had not yet arrived; and he returned to his labour rather crest-fallen. For myself, my ambition prompted me to aspire to the rack (another part of the refining process) but to that dignity I was never promoted."

* * * * * * * * * * *

Samuel's mother died shortly after he started work at the stamps, and 'in the second year of his widowhood' his father remarried. Samuel was then sent, at the age of ten and a half, as apprentice to a shoemaker. He would never return to work at the mines.

* * * * * * * * * * *

John Harris (1820-82)

John Harris was born nearly half a century after Samuel, at Six Chimneys, in the hamlet of Bolenowe (a few miles south of Camborne) on 14th October 1820. As with Samuel, he was born into a Methodist mining family. Similarly, the wages from mining were rarely enough to support a family, and so his father John also needed to supplement his income by farming a smallholding.

John was sent to a series of small dame schools and eventually became fairly proficient in the three R's before beginning his working life, at the age of nine, but that was the extent of his formal education. His first work was as a plough boy, with his uncle. However, after a few months he went to work at a tin stream out on Forest Moor, between Bolenowe and Four Lanes. Then, at ten years old, he went to work at surface at Dolcoath. Although John does not describe his work at surface, he was probably employed at picking over the ores in the first instance (a vital training in identification for all would-be miners) and then sent to the buddles after a few months. (The other main task allocated to boys at the copper mines at this time was jigging, but this was generally reserved for older boys).

It was here, on the dressing floors, that John's poetic talent was first publicly observed, when he was encouraged to recite his creations during lunch breaks. He very soon became, in his own words, a '*compulsive writer of rhymes'*. His main sources of inspiration were the land, the people and the natural world he saw around him.

After two years at surface, John followed his father underground at Dolcoath. He was to continue working there for twenty-four years, until his health began to fail. Having been a Sunday School teacher at Troon since the age of sixteen, he was then offered a post as Scripture Reader at a mission in Falmouth, from 1857. He continued at this work for over twenty-five years, until shortly before he died. During all these years at both Dolcoath and in Falmouth, he continued to compile his poems.

Fig. 3 Portrait of John Harris
Courtesy of the Cornish Centre Collection

His first published book was *'Lays from Mine, Moor and Mountain'* in 1853, followed by *'The Mountain Prophet, The Mine and Other Poems'* in 1860. *'The Story of Carn Brea, Essays and Poems'* was written in 1863, and he won the prize offered by Coventry Town Council for the tercentenary of Shakespeare's birth, with an *'Ode to Shakespeare'*. Other books of poems followed, and he finally published *'My Biography'* in 1882. He died on 7th Jan 1884, and is buried in Treslothan churchyard.

* * * * * * * * * * * *

Reproduced below, are the passages from his autobiography where John remembers, firstly, his work at the tin streams on Forest Moor and, secondly, his time at surface at Dolcoath. Also included are those parts of his poems which are clearly inspired by these experiences. *'Copper and Tin'* is this word-artist's impression of the different colours, textures and forms of the minerals with which he worked. This poem seems to have been published in its own right, as well as part of his remarkable poem *'The Mine'*. In *'The Mine'*, Harris draws a picture of the history of Cornish metal mining across the centuries. The two excerpts chosen here describe the birth of simple technology in the early tin streams and, in stark contrast, the noisy and busy surface scene of the deep mines of his youth. (Dolcoath, where Harris worked, was the largest mine in Cornwall, at the time). Finally, included here is a fascinating glossary of mining terms, which John Harris compiled for his autobiography.

* * * * * * * * * * *

My Autobiography
John Harris
(selected passages)

'At nine years of age I was taken from school and put to work in the fields, to drive the horses in the plough to Uncle Harris, Bolenowe....I do not recollect writing any rhymes whilst with Uncle George, partly because I was kept so busy, and partly because I was with him only a few months, nor do I remember whether I had any payment in the shape of wages for the long day's work, save the dinner of cold meat and roast potatoes.'

'I then went to work with an old tin-streamer of the name of Waters. One day we discovered a Jews'-house[3] in the bog. The tin had run over their smelting pot and had lodged in the turf, which had occurred, it is supposed, hundreds of years before the birth of Christ.'[4]

'The old tin-streamer gave me threepence a day to throw sand from the river in Forest Moor. Here I stood with bare feet in the running water, with a small shovel in my hands, and ate my dinner in a peat-built, rush-covered hut. The tinkle of the silver brook, the sigh of the wind through the white tufted rushes, the birds singing on the willow branches, or floating carelessly through the air revived the suppressed spirit of numbers never again to sink into repose.'[5]

'At ten years of age my father took me with him to Dolcoath Mine, to work at the surface, in assisting to dress and prepare the copper ore, for the market. I used frequently to repeat the rhymes I had written to my mates in the mine. They would put me to stand on a hand-barrow by the cobbing-house door, or on a heap of minerals on the floors, and then gather round me to hear my verses. It was not unpleasant for me to hear them conversing with each other, while the jingle of my last lay was in their ears, 'What a wonderful boy that is! He can read a book like a parson.'[6]

* * * * * * * * * * *

---

[3] An ancient Blowing House (a simple tin smelter)
[4] The tin was collected and sold at Hayle for £37
[5] pp. 33-34
[6] pp. 36-37

8

Copper and Tin

Copper has colours different in the ores,
As various as the rainbow – black and blue
And green and red and yellow as a flower;
Gold-coloured here, there dimly visible,
Though rich the same in measure and in meed.
'Tis found alike where glittering granite gloams,
Where killas darkens, and where gossens shroud
And oft where wise ones write it cannot be –
Thus wisely scattered by the Hand Divine.
Tin is more secret far, with duller eye
Oft hiding in the river's shingly bed,
Or in the flint's bosom, near the central fires,
In chambers wide, or veins like silken lace,
So that the labourer, stumbling on a start,
Wipes his hot brow, and cries, "Lo, here is tin."

The Mine Part II

'Each day the lode grew richer, and more tin
Was lying on the surface. Then he made
A wooden wheel, and placed it in the wall,
And on some stakes of oak put iron heads,
To stamp the rough stones into powder fine
Then o'er the wheal he turned the limped stream,
And round it went, up rose the heavy heads,
And falling bruised the stones to mineral sand.'

The Mine Part I

9

'A mine spreads out its vast machinery.
Here engines, with their huts and smokey stacks,
Cranks, wheels, and rods, boilers and hissing steam,
Pressed up the water from the depths below.
Here fire-whims ran till almost out of breath,
And chains cried sharply, strained with fiery force.
Here blacksmiths hammered by the sooty forge,
And there a crusher crashed the copper ore.
Here girls were cobbing under roofs of straw,
And there were giggers at the oaken hutch.
Here a man-engine glided up and down,
A blessing and a boon to mining men:
And near the spot where, many years before,
Turned round and round the rude old water-wheel,
A huge fire-stamps was working evermore,
And slimey boys were swarming at the trunks.
The noisy lander by the trap-door bawled
With pincers in his hand; and troops of maids
With heavy hammers brake the mineral stones.
The cart-man cried, and shook his broken whip;
And on the steps of the account-house stood
The active agent, with his eye on all'.

The Mine Part II

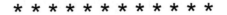

Glossary of Mining Terms

(from *My Autobiography*, by John Harris)

COBBING HOUSE   Where the mineral is cobbed, or
                        beaten, from the dead stones.

FLOORS   The space assigned to the dressed
                        ores, when prepared for the
                        market.

HUTCH	Where the fine ores are sifted in water, and prepared for the market.
KEEVE	A hooped barrel, half-filled with water, where the rough mineral is washed in a sieve.
MAN-ENGINE	A machine to let the workman up and down the mine.
PICKING TABLE	Where the valuable ores are picked out, and the refuse thrown away.
PLOT	An excavation in the side of the shaft, having a floor of wood, where the broken earth is shovelled into a bucket.
SINK	A kind of well.
SLIDE	The compartment where the mineral is trammed when drawn to the surface.
TIN-STOPE	A stair-cut excavation over or under a level.
TRIBUTER	One who labours for a certain portion of the mineral he may discover.

* * * * * * * * * * *

Bibliography

Drew, Samuel (jnr.) *Samuel Drew, the Self-Taught Cornishman: A Life Lesson* (Ward 1861)

Harris, John *My Autobiography* (London 1882)

Harris, John *Wayside Pictures, Hymns and Poems* (Hamilton Adams 1874)

Newman, Paul *The Meads of Love; The Life and Poetry of John Harris (1820-84)* (Dyllansow Truran 1994)

Thomas, D. H. (Ed.) *Songs from the Earth: Selected Poems of John Harris, Cornish Miner, 1820-84* (Lodenek Press 1977)

Wilkinson, John T. *Samuel Drew 1765-1833* (CMHA Occasional Paper No. 5)

Chapter 2

The Story of Patty Tremelling

A tiny booklet, no more than three inches by one and a half, published in 1841, tells the retrospective story of Patty, who died in 1837 at the age of 33. (See Fig. 4) The book is called '*Patty Tremellin: the Life of a Cornish Mine Girl Written by Herself*'. At first glance it appears to be a fictitious 'improving novel', to be an inspiration and warning to other young women, written sometimes in the first person, sometimes in the third. However, the book lacks the flow and structure of a novel, indicating that it might actually be a compilation of real life events. Subsequent research of parish registers for Redruth, St Mewan, St Ewe and St Austell matches numerous events within the story, and almost certainly indicates that Patty Tremelling is the central character. It seems that the book was written after her death, based on a journal she began to write during her final illness, and on conversations she had with the author of the book. We do not know who the author was, but it may be either her local minister or the curate at Wrestling Green, St Austell, both of whom had supported Patty in her final years.

Fig. 4 Photograph reproduced by kind permission of The Royal Institution of Cornwall

The booklet is certainly written for 'religious inspiration' with longish tracts of early Victorian theology, but the story line is one of both tragedy and courage. We read of a young woman who had been raised in the old Cornish custom of 'keeping company' i.e. engaging in sexual activity with her betrothed, on the understanding that marriage would ensue if and when she became pregnant. Unfortunately, this does not happen and Patty is left abandoned with her children. On her encounter with the evangelical and conservative church and chapel doctrines of the early 19th century, she finds herself torn with remorse and self-loathing, but eventually finds a way to some spiritual peace within herself. Most of the account is written in the first person (as if from her journal) although some of these passages have more of the feel of a well-practised sermon than coming from the pen of a woman with limited schooling. Other passages are clearly written by her posthumous biographer.

Although a few sequences of Patty's biographical story do not coincide with the formal records, the majority of them do. The book appears to be based on the life of Martha Patience Tremelling (Tremellun, Tremellyn, Tremelline or Tremellin). Her parents were Francis and Martha Tremelling, and her baptism was recorded at St Uny Parish Church, Redruth on 18th March 1804. Her father was a miner, and her parents seem to have come from the St Ewe and St Austell area, originally. Her poverty-stricken parents sent her, at an early age, to live with a series of aunts, one of whom was able to give her a rudimentary education. It became obvious from these limited opportunities that Patty was very intelligent, and quick to learn. As a teenager she was called back to her estranged family (now in St Austell), to help care for an ailing mother and her younger siblings. In addition, she was sent to work as an ore dresser at the local mine. Soon after, all of the working members of the family were thrown out of work when the mine closed (this may have been Wheal Hewas, which ceased production in 1822). This created an even greater financial crisis for the family, and Patty left home to find mining work elsewhere. These next few years were to be far from happy for Patty. During this time, she was to give birth to three illegitimate children, suffer from severe depression, be twice detained in Bodmin Gaol, and eventually become terminally ill.

She clearly associated her pregnancies with relationships that were formed at the mine. Her first child was probably Richard Bray Tremellen, who was baptised at St Austell Parish Church on 6th June 1830, and is recorded as '*b.*[1] *son of Patience Tremellen*'. The St Ewe overseers accounts record that she received £1 6s on Lady Day 1929, for her child, from John Bray.[2] Her second son appears to be William Thomas, born in the summer of 1831, when Patty was 27 years old. Subsequently, Patty was committed to the County Gaol in Bodmin on 5th October 1831; her book records that it was for a small debt, but the admissions register

---

[1] Base (ie. illegitimate) son
[2] St Ewe Parish Overseers Accounts 1795-1884 (CRO: P62/12)

states it was for *'disobeying an order of bastardy to satisfy the parish of St Ewe'* (i.e. not naming the father of her child). What pressure was brought to bear, or what fear she had of naming the father, we do not know. She was sentenced to three months imprisonment or was to pay a fine of £1 0s 10d. (It was possibly this fine that was described as the *'small debt'*). The Bodmin Admissions Register for 1831 movingly gives a physical description of her: height 5'3", grey eyes, brown hair, oval face with pale pockmarked complexion. Her behaviour was recorded as orderly.[3] She was discharged early, on 13th December 1831, and the St Ewe overseers record her receiving about £3 per year from a John Luke, from 1831 until 1835, for a second child.

Patty's third child, John Francis, was baptised on 29th April 1832 at St Ewe Parish Church, where he was recorded as *'bastard child of Martha Tremelling (servant)'*. She was once again committed to jail for refusing to divulge the name of the father. An entry in the Bodmin Quarter Sessions of 1833 reads: *'2nd July: Martha Tremellen, St Ewe. For refusing to name father. To remain in custody.'* [4] She was released early, in November 1833, as she had become seriously ill. She was never to regain her health. It seems that her middle child, William, was not baptised until 30th Sept 1834 (at St Ewe Parish Church) where he is described as *'almost three years old'*, and the *'bastard of Martha Tremelline, servant'*.

During her time in Bodmin Goal, Patty had been visited by Quakers and encouraged to help teach other inmates to read. Once back home, the Quakers continued their contact, and Patty was also visited by the local curate and members of the Methodist society. Her faith began to deepen, and she started to record her own story in a journal. She was confined to bed for nearly three years, during which time her health gradually deteriorated.

Her death is among the first recorded with the General Register Office for England and Wales, as it had only been made a legal requirement a few weeks before. Her death certificate, issued on the 4th November, in the sub-district of St Austell, reads: *'October 10: Martha Tremellen 33 years spinster.'* The cause of death is given as consumption, and Patty's mother, Martha, was the informant who had been present, as the book describes, at her death. She was buried in the St Austell Parish Church burial ground, and the register simply reads: *'12th October 1837: Martha Tremellen aged 33 of Wrestling Downs, bed lier [sic] for 3 years.'* In her final years, before her tragic death, however, Patty had come to find

---

[3] Bridewell Admissions Book (CRO: AD 1676/1/2 Entry 6605)
[4] Bodmin Quarter Sessions (CRO: QSI 12/300)

peace with herself, and used her own educational abilities to teach the children from her local community.

* * * * * * * * * * * * * * * * *

Patty Tremellin; The Life of a Cornish Mine Girl

Written by Herself

Patty Tremullin, the subject of these memoirs, was the daughter of a Cornish miner and was born at Redruth in the year 1804. When she was two years old she was kindly taken charge of by her aunt, living in Penzance. With reference to this period of her life she writes, '*my kind friends were very tender over me, and I loved them; they put me to school when very young, and kept me there till I was able to work at my needle pretty well.*' Afterwards she went to a writing school till she was eight years old, then her uncle took her to assist him in his shop. She proceeds, '*My kind friends put me to an evening school, where I improved very fast in my learning. This pleasing scene lasted till I was nine years old, but I feel sorry to relate my happy hours soon fled – my dear aunt becoming very ill, and old age having overtaken her, she thought it prudent to put me again under dear mother's care. I did not anticipate at that time it would be such an unspeakable loss as it soon proved, for not having seen my father for the space of seven years, I knew not the love of father or mother, although I felt glad I was going to St Austell, where my parents resided. My benefactors parted with me very reluctantly, but my mother kindly received me and I ever found her a kind and loving parent.*' After remaining with her parents for about a year, Patty was again sent for by her aunt who had recovered from her late illness.

She says, '*My kind friends gladly received me and put me to school again; my schoolmistress gave me a good character for learning. My dear aunt delighted in reading the scriptures, and would often say it was a comfort to her to hear me read the Bible so well at my age. Her weakness being now almost insupportable, and her dissolution fast approaching, my kind friends once again thought it right for me to return to my parents. How transitory are the scenes of earthly happiness in the time spent in the delightful situation at Penzance swiftly passed away like most of the enjoyment here on earth. I never saw my dear aunt more. Soon after my mother was sent for to come to her before she closed her eyes in death. Our dear aunt left a clear testimony behind her that she* was going to glory; she told my mother even the hour when she expected her spirit to take flight; on hearing the clock strike that hour, she said, 'It is accomplished – I am going to Jesus,' and then fell asleep in Jesus. Soon after my return from Penzance, my father's sister wished to take me, and my parents consented to let me go, she being a widow, and having no child. My aunt was a Methodist, and had been one of that society about 40 years, and now at the age of four score and six she still is able to attend her class-meeting. My kind aunt gave me good instructions, but the following account will show how I slighted them.'

'I remained with this aunt two years, my mother's family being increased, she thought it proper to take me home to look after the younger children. I lived with my parents until I was 16, when I went to work at the mines; my father's wages at the time were small, my mother was very ill, our family large, and corn dear, so that both my father and mother had to go to work without meat. Many days we had nothing but boiled greens to make use of. I had 3 miles to go to work every morning, and all the work of the house to do after my return at night, as my poor mother was laid up of a cancer. My work at the mines got very scarce, and at last I could get nothing to do, many beside me being thrown out of employment.'

'Those mines are bad places for boys and girls, for there is nothing but sin to be heard or witnessed all day long, when the agents are out of the way'. Under her trying circumstances, Patty endeavoured to go to her uncle's in Penzance, from where she had in former days experienced so much kindness – without money and almost without food, it may be readily conceived that her journey was performed with much suffering. At Truro she was kindly furnished with food and lodging by an acquaintance of her mother's, and after passing a sleepless night there she pursued her tedious journey on foot the following morning. 'I went on' she says, 'without interruption; how wonderfully the Lord protected me on the way, but I could not see it came from God. I do not remember having experienced any thankful feeling to God for all his goodness to me on the journey. About this time I left my parents an account of my work being so far from where they lived – hundreds of times I have regretted that step'.

'O Lord! Enable me to begin to write the horrors of seduction! I know without help I cannot do it; shame will overpower me, and Satan will try to hinder me. Oh! If I had a virtuous life to write, it does not appear that my pen would not stand reluctant in my fingers; but I have an encouragement to write; our gracious Lord has said , 'I come not to call the righteous, but sinners of repentance' – and we are assured that all who truly repent of their sins shall be forgiven.'

'Soon after this I gave myself to company, and frequented the dancing room; I was never satisfied with dancing and often have stayed until 10 or 11 o'clock. This exposes young women to great temptation, which I found to my sorrow, although I escaped many times the bait which Satan had laid before me. I became deeply attached to a young man to whom I thought I could have sacrificed everything, and who had often promised marriage. Oh! How I have grieved and lamented to think on the hour I listened to the voice of temptation! Soon after, he deserted me, and I was left to bewail my condition and lament my fall. When nearing my confinement my father ordered me to leave his house; - this went to my heart, but after I got a place to go to, with a very sober woman, about half a mile from our house'.

'After this I was ill nine months, so that I was not able to go out of doors, it was trouble that kept me so weak. I thought if I was permitted to recover, I would live close to God, but this resolution was made in my own strength. Three years and six months from this time I fell into the same gross sin again. How merciful the Lord was to my soul, that he did not cut me off, and cast me into that place where hope can never come'.

'Satan now began to work in me stronger than ever; fearing my parents would get to know of my situation, and that I should be turned out of doors, I was determined to go home and destroy myself. I was so hardened that I felt no fear of a future punishment. A religious young woman with whom I worked told me afterwards she saw something in my countenance that was not right, but she said nothing to me about it then. I soon reached my parents door; there was no-one within; I went in, fully bent on this wicked purpose. I took down a razor from the cupboard, intending to cut my throat, but oh! how wonderfully the Lord prevented this wicked intent. The young woman before mentioned having followed me, entered the house. I concealed the razor, wishing in my mind she was gone, but she waited till my mother saw me. She asked me what was the matter, I looked so ill. I was very reluctant to disclose my situation, but my mother insisted on me telling her, which I did, but said nothing of my wicked intent. My dear mother said I would break her heart, to think what I had brought myself to, and that I was a disgrace to the family. I thought I would soon put an end to this. There was a cow-house near, and I thought if I could get there I would hang myself. Many times during the evening I endeavoured to make my escape, but my mother followed me, and persuaded me to come in and go to bed. I went with her, but Satan would not let me rest. I then took the razor and carried it to bed with me. I placed it under my pillow, and thought to commit the deed when all the house was quiet; but I had not been in bed many minutes before my mother came and told me to give up the razor. I denied that I had it, but she searched the bed and found it. She then began to weep, and told my father what was the matter. My father said he should have me confined. He then asked my mother how she knew I had the razor; she said the Lord must have put it into her mind to rise from her seat and see if it was removed from its usual place, and when she found it was gone, she thought she would have sunk into the earth. I felt worse than ever, because I had not done it before. My mother then began to point out the sufferings that Satan would inflict on me after he had me in his power; this I believed but then I thought I should be out of everyone's sight, for I was ashamed to be seen. I had no rest for months afterward; Satan was still tempting me to commit self-murder. I did not pray to God against it, but I felt fear of the punishment. I was afraid if I prayed, the Lord would strike me dead. Soon after this all fear was taken from me. My mother began to talk with me after the rest of the family had gone to bed, saying what I had brought myself to, and that I was killing her with trouble. I began to cry to think I how I had grieved my poor mother – it was near midnight. I went out and wandered up and down in the field by myself, or I should have said Satan with me. There was a deep shaft (a pit through which the miners bring up the ore) in the field. I went and stood on the brink of the shaft to plunge myself in it. It was very deep and many fathoms of water in it. I was struck with trembling whilst standing on the brink of the shaft, and I seemed to be on the verge of hell, when my mind was impressed as if a voice spoke to me, that it was better to go back to be laughed at by everyone, than to go to hell, for I might still repent. I was struck with such fear that I could neither move backwards, nor forwards for some time. My poor mother was in search of me, I went towards her, but was not willing to go into the house; she spoke to me very kindly, for she felt for my distress.'

'Soon after this, being near my confinement, my parents told me I must leave the house. I went and got a place with two old people, who were both religious; they took pity on me, and said I should stay with them until I was confined. While I remained with them I worked at my needle to support myself; I then put my child out to nurse, and, paid my part as long as I was able; but being taken ill I could not do it any longer. I was then committed to Bodmin prison for 3 months, for a small debt, but I was liberated before that time expired. Whilst in prison I was tempted not to return to my home anymore, for I thought I should be spurned by everyone; but I thought on the good advice the visiting ladies at the prison gave me. I used to read a great deal, and teach such of the other female prisoners as were willing to be taught.'

'*After my return home, I kept myself from all company, until I went to work at the mine, when I gave myself to company again: but I was never easy in my mind, for I always felt afraid the Lord would strike me dead in the midst of my sins. I was the greater sinner for this, because I was sinning against light and knowledge. It is indeed a mercy of mercies that I am still in time! Sometimes I am ready to drop my pen and not write anymore, for I am ashamed of my own self. I am sure I should never do it but for the encouragement of those who in a like manner have gone astray, should any such ever meet with these lines; knowing that if we truly repent of our sins, we shall obtain salvation through the blood and saving merits of our blessed Redeemer; therefore my blackest deeds I hope to pen, for God knoweth all.*'

'*The third time I brought myself to shame, I did not want for anything in a temporal sense; but I was very ill for a long time.*' Soon after this she was committed to Bodmin Prison for refusing to name the father of her child. Her sufferings whilst there she describes. '*After I had been in Bodmin prison some weeks, I was taken very ill and brought up a quantity of blood. The doctor was sent for immediately, and I was bled; I was so weak that I could not walk or speak, and the female prisoners carried me to bed. I have cause to be thankful for the kindness of the Governor, the surgeon, and the matron as well as the visiting ladies and the chaplain. I have wondered many times how the Lord was so kind to me, when I would not be kind to myself; the chaplain died a few weeks ago; (1835). He died clear of my blood, for he warned me to flee from the wrath to come. At last the quarter sessions came, and the Governor told me I must prepare to go before the justices. I thought I should have swooned away. There were many prisoners both male and female, to be put up with me; the others were mostly for felony. I never held up my head all the way going through the town; I was ready to sink with trouble.*' She was remanded for prison for the same as before, but was liberated a few weeks after and returned to St. Austell where, in about 20 months she was visited with a severe illness. She proceeds, '*no tongue can tell what my feelings were when I was taken down on the bed of affliction; no language can express it. It could not bear the thoughts of death, for when I reflected on a future punishment, I thought mine must be very great. Satan would sometimes suggest to me, for when I seemed to do a little better, my thoughts would be like a fool's eye, wandering to the end of the world. My first confinement to my bed, was in the last month of the year 1833. When I kept my bed about a month, after which I was able to come downstairs again. It was then I hoped I should get better, but those hopes, the Lord in mercy took from me, and showed me my dangerous state; for I was still getting worse in body, and my mind was like a troubled sea, that is always casting up mire and dirt; but to no-one could I unburden my grief; for I knew I had brought my trouble on myself. I was afraid to read my Bible, lest it should condemn me; but the Lord's dealing towards me were full of mercy. He first deprived me of health, and then of my temporal food; but one day, as I was sitting downstairs, being so weak that I could not walk without help, and having had nothing to make use of but cold water for the day. I thought I should sink under my burden; as I was crying and lamenting my condition, I heard a horse stop at my door, and a gentleman's voice calling my mother; this made me tremble in every limb. I stood much in fear of this gentleman; he had called to inquire after my health, or I might say the Lord had sent him. I was so much ashamed of my conduct when this kind gentleman came in, seeing that I could not speak to him, he kindly said, 'Do not alarm yourself, I am not going to say anything of the past, but read your Bible like a good creature' – he saw I was very ill, but I did not let him know how I was circumstanced, although I had nothing to make use of; but blessed be for ever to the Lord for his kindness to such a vile wretch as I am; when this kind gentleman was about to leave, he placed a piece of money on the table. I was overcome when I saw the kindness of the gentlemen, and the goodness of the Lord in sending him to me; that I had scarcely power to thank him. From that time I took to my Bible, but how dark its content seemed to me! For many months every passage seemed to confound me; I thought the day of grace was past. I dwelt much on these words 'ye have set at nought all my counsel and would have none of my reproof; I also will laugh at your calamity; I will mock when your fear cometh'. I thought this was my state, for I was now praying to the Lord to forgive my sins, yet I did not believe he would do it. My fear was come, but I hoped I had none. At this time I was in so much pain that I could not lie down in bed, but oh! The anguish of my soul, oh! No words can express! My doctor and my friends, as well as myself, thought death had taken hold of me; I lost my speech, and the use of my limbs, but not my senses; my mother was much alarmed, and called my father and one of our neighbours; it was about midnight. I heard them say 'she is dying'. Had I died then, I should have gone to dwell with the prince of darkness for ever; but although my lips could not utter a word, my heart was saying, 'Lord spare me! Save me'. I continued in this state for many hours. When morning came I was able to speak. My eldest brother asked if he should fetch someone to pray with me; I told him I should be glad if he could, he went to many places, but no-one came. I thought if someone would come and pray for me, the Lord might hear their prayer on my behalf. At last a class leader among the Methodists came to see me; he inquired after the state of my mind; I told him I was miserable; I was not sensible long together; he prayed with me, and whilst he was praying I roared as a lion, for the disquieting of my heart, he stopped in his prayer and said 'What can be done in this case? I should think she would not live through the night.' He took my weak hand in his, and said, 'I will call to see you tomorrow morning'. I did not sleep for the night, wishing for the*

Sunday morning to come; but this poor man did not keep to his promise, for I did not see him again until many months after; the reason he did not come was he thought it was too late. Now I was cast down more than ever, and my pain of body was so great that I was oft times ready to cry out 'It is more than I am able to bear'. Soon after this, two ladies belonging to the Society of Friends came to our door to inquire whether we wanted a Bible and said we might have one by paying a penny a week until the price was made up. My brother said we had a Bible, and then he asked those ladies if they would like to step upstairs to see his sister who was very ill. When I saw them come into the room I began to cry; they asked what was the matter; I told them I was a great sinner and wanted pardon, but I was too weak to speak much. One of the ladies said, 'It may not be so far from thee as thou mayest suppose' and directed me to the 1st chapter Isaiah 18th v. 'Come now, and let us reason together, saith the Lord, though your sins are scarlet; they shall be as white as snow; though they be red like crimson, they shall be as wool'. This gave me encouragement. These dear ladies left two blessings behind them; and one of them told me she would come again, which she kindly did the next day. She didn't know what manner of life I had led, and I thought that if she had known it, she would not have so kind as to visit me again. It was a great cross to disclose it to her, she said 'Christ did not come to call the righteous, but the sinners to repentance'. My spirit felt animated whilst she was speaking of goodness of God. Very soon, after this, a man came to our house, a stranger to all of us; he was a preacher among the Primitive Methodists; he prayed with me, and urged the necessity of me laying hold by faith, but I could not feel to say it, for I thought if I said what I did not feel, the Lord would never receive me. When the Lord first spoke peace and got my soul, it was in the night, when all the family were fast asleep, that I felt relieved of my burden. I seemed to be as light as a feather, and I could rejoice in God – as for the pain of my body – I felt none. I thought I would wake my mother, and tell her the blessing I had found, but a thought struck me directly that I had better keep it to myself, lest I should be deceiving myself. This made Satan tremble to think he was about to lose such a faithful servant, one who had served him so many years. At last I woke my mother, and told her what the Lord had done for my soul. When I think on the infinite condescension of my blessed Redeemer, I am lost in wonder, love and praise for his great kindness, on sparing such a rebel as I – the chief of sinners – a disgrace to the female sex. I am now led to cry out, 'Lord, is it possible I am still in time?'. Amazing love! Lord, what is man that thou art mindful of him, or the son of man that thou thus visitest him! The scripture tells us that the Lord Jesus is the propitiation for our sins, and died an ignominious death upon the cross, that through him we might have eternal life. We are bought with the price of his blood, and as many as believe on the Lord Jesus Christ shall be saved. Christ calls for all to come to this fountain and be cleansed. It was for our sins that Christ came forth from the Father to be stripped of his glory, to take on him the human form! How thankful ought we to be for this unspeakable gift! Unfathomable love! He is an advocate and Redeemer! He forever stands at the right hand of the Father interceding for us; and by his blood we are redeemed, we are justified by his merits, and sanctified by his Holy Spirit! These blessings are as free for us as the air we breathe. If we stop short of this blessing, the fault is not in Christ. It must be by faith that we shall receive it – without faith it is impossible to please God. It is not by works, lest any man should boast. Then are we not to pray? Yes – 'pray without ceasing'. But when we pray it should be in faith, believing that whatever we ask in the name of Jesus, will be granted; for the Christian would ask nothing, more than what he believed would be for the glory of God. The scripture says, 'Now is the day of salvation'. It is said today – not tomorrow 'now is the appointed time' - there is no promise for tomorrow.'

'The more we look to the scriptures the more delight we shall find in them; they are so full of sweet promises; and we must hang on them by faith. There is a promise for everyone. Ha! Everyone that thirsteth, come ye to the waters; and he that hath no money, come buy and eat; buy wine and milk, without money and without price. How can we neglect so great a salvation? When we take the blessed book in our hands to read, we must pray to God to seek us; we must become as little children, and the Lord will teach us by his Holy Spirit, that we might behold wonderful things out of his law. If we desire to be freed from bondage, we must seek it from Him who is exalted, a Prince and a Saviour, to give repentance and forgiveness of sin. Blessed are all they, and only they, who put their trust in him. I was for many years seeking my own torment when I might have been seeking my own comfort – working hard to go to hell. 'If these lines should fall under the notice of any poor female who has gone astray as I have, I would entreat her to forsake her evil ways and beg of God forgiveness. Depend on it the Lord will take you in,; none need despair since I have found mercy. We have heard of many poor creatures who have been taken off in a most deplorable condition. I think it right to mention a case that fell to my notice sometime after I was confined to my bed. A poor female, through bad conduct, had brought herself to the lowest ebb; she had for many years lived in the ways of sin, when the Lord was pleased to afflict her with a paralytic stroke, which so disabled her that she could not help herself; she was taken too the workhouse, and after a short time the Lord raised her up again, when she left the workhouse, and went on sinning as before. A kind lady who had often talked seriously to her, met her in her walk, and begged her to leave her sinful ways, and made her promise to visit me; when she came I received her as a sister. I entreated her to leave off her sinful ways; but my words did not appear to have much effect on her. Soon after she was seized a second time with a paralytic stroke, and again sent to the workhouse; when she was better, she came again to my house, and remained there three weeks, during which time, I read and talked to her, and entreated her to pray whilst she had the power; but she said it was no use, for she knew she would go to hell. She was seized a third time, sent to the workhouse and in a few days expired! The Lord has opened the door to receive the publican and the harlot, if we will only fall at the feet of Jesus to be cleansed by his precious blood. We must cry out with the publicans of old, 'God be merciful to me, a sinner'. We must pray to God to make us humble – we can never do this of ourselves. Satan may suggest that we must do better before we can come to God, or else he will never accept us. Until the Lord is pleased to show us that, we are nothing better, but still going worse. When at last, Satan comes in a flood, and tells us it is too late; he will try to deceive us unto the end, for he was a deceiver from the beginning. Satan cannot bear to lose one of his subjects, but angels rejoice to see such sinners such as we are coming to God. 'There is more joy over one sinner who repenteth more than over ninety nine just persons who need no repentance'. My daily prayer is that sinners may be brought to God. May this prayer be answered for the sake of Jesus Christ our Redeemer.'

During a long illness Patty was accustomed to commit her experiences to paper; and the state of her mind during this period will be shown by the following extracts from her journal; 1835. 'O thou great fountain of felicity, from whom I derive all my comfort, I bless thy name for the manifold blessing thou hast bestowed upon me. I do not deserve of favour from thy hand, but in thy mercy and loving kindness thou hast given me many. I thank thee, of Father of goodness, for sending the curate of this parish to me this day. I felt my spirit animated whilst he was speaking of the goodness of God, and his son Jesus Christ, and his comforting Spirit; and reading the 14th chapter of John, he dwelt much on these words of Christ, 'Peace I leave with you, my peace give I unto you; not as the world giveth I unto you. Let not your heart be troubled, neither let it be afraid'. This encourages my soul to press forward, to run that race which is before me with unwearied diligence. It is now one year and nine months since I was confined to my bed, O Lord! Still keep me and guide me in that oath of life everlasting – Amen. Amen.'

'O Lord! I beseech thee, enable me to write in the deepest humility, and instruct me with thy Holy Spirit, that whatever I do, I may do to thy glory. It is through mercy that thou hast afflicted me. The curate was very kind yesterday in sending me a book, entitled 'The Dairyman's Daughter'. I found it a very interesting work. It made tears of joy run down my face, to think how she and her aged parents expressed themselves for the kindness of the clergyman in visiting them. O thou most blessed Parent *of good, give me a double portion of her spirit'. O Lord! Enable me always to remember our kind curate at the throne of grace! Oh! Bless him for entering my abode. Gird him with thy strength, and let him follow thee through evil report as well as good report, for thou art his help and his shield.'*

'I am spared through mercy, to see the light of another day, but still very weak; although much revived since last night – I then thought my spirit would have taken it's flight to brighter worlds above. I found it sweet to lie as passive clay in the hands of the potter; And I could say through the strength of the Lord, 'not as I will, but as thou wilt.' 'O Lord! Thou art my God; I will exalt thee; I will praise thy name, for thou hast done wonderful things; thy counsels of old are faithfulness and truth.' I do bless the Lord for sending the kind ladies from the Society of Friends to my house. This day I received my Bible, after subscribing for many months – the price was 5s 8d. This money I have not found wanting, but my Bible I hope to find a great treasure. Many other blessings those kind ladies have sent to me this day – may the Lord reward them for their kindness to me, who am not worthy of the least favour. I want to feel more love to my Saviour: I often think my breathings are not ardent enough to him that numbereth the whole;

> *'Much of love I ought to know, since I have been so much forgiven.'*

'This week I seen much of the goodness of God, having been highly favoured by some visits by the Society of Friends, who have been very kind to me; they were the first people that visited me after I was confined to my bed. I was then in distress – both of body and soul - they kindly supported the wants of the body, and directed me to rely on the merits of Jesus for salvation. My prayer is that the Lord may reward them.'

'How thankful I feel to God for this interval of ease, which enables me to take my pen and write in my weak hand, once more to write of his goodness towards my soul. The sufferings that I have gone through since I wrote last, no-one knows, but God; my body has been sore afflicted, but my soul is wonderfully supported. The Lord has sweetened all my pains, for he has said, - I will not lay on thee more than thou art able to bear – praise be to his name for ever! I want to devote my breath to God, and the language of my heart is;

> *'Sink down my soul, sink lower still, lie loved with the dust.'*

'I ought to praise God with every breath I draw, for his loving kindness to me is more than the tongue can express. Since I last wrote, I have

undergone a surgical operation. I was supported in a wonderful manner, praise be the Lord for giving such strength. I do not know how my doctor was going to be paid, but I was not long left with thoughts like these; for the Lord sent a good friend to me, who kindly said, 'I will pay your doctor for you.' May the Lord render him a double portion to him for his kindness to one so unworthy;

'Thou, O Lord, in tender love, dost all my burdens bear,
Oh! Lift my heart to things above, and fix it ever there!'

'Since I last wrote, I have had a severe bilious attack. I was for many days depressed in Spirit, but not dismayed. I waited in the Lord, and found it good to wait. My soul cries out in a rapture of love;

'What are my sufferings here, if thou Lord, makest me meet
With that enraptured host to appear, and worship at thy feet.'

Yesterday I brought leanness in my soul by conversing too freely with a person not religious, who came to my room. The things of the world began to divert my attention too much; my daily prayer is to feel dead to the things of this world, and truly alive unto God. I feel worldly company a great destroyer to the soul. I do praise the Lord for his goodness towards my soul, and I hope I shall be able to praise him as long as life will last. I have been very ill these two weeks past, one evening last week, when very weak in the body, the Lord enabled my to draw my weak frame to the window; the horizon very clear, and the moon beautifully gave her light to illuminate the earth; the labourer was gone to his rest; the noise and bustle of the day were over; everything was quiet, peaceful and serene; I glanced my eye towards the heavens; how beautiful the clouds appeared as I viewed them passing and re-passing by the command of God, thought I, those clouds might well reproach me for my disobedience. I was ashamed of myself, and prayed that the Lord would make me more humble, and increase my desire after him, and truly my desire is, to love God, with all my heart, with all my mind, with all my soul, and with all my strength; for I know that God is a jealous God – he cannot bear a rival.'

'Every moment, Lord, I want the merit of thy death.'

The forgoing extracts exhibit that deep humiliation and contrition of a soul which the subject of these memoirs experienced in contemplating the sinful course of her past life; and they also bear evidence, that, having come out of great tribulation, she was, through redeeming love and mercy, made sensible that her past transgressions had been blotted out, and her sins forgiven, and therefore her language was that of praise, and her feeling those of love to him who had dealt so bountifully with her; she loved much, for she had had much forgiven. But her conduct also evinced that the language she used was the language of the heart.

When capable of exertion she had several children collected in her bedroom, whom she instructed in reading and needlework; and her little school was valued by those whose children were privileged to attend it: she also partly supported herself by needlework, when the state of her health [sic], but for several weeks before her death her bodily sufferings were so great that she was unable to attend to her little school. During this time of protracted weakness she was preserved in much patience. Her interest for the best welfare of the different members of her family was evident: not long before her death she earnestly entreated her sister *'Do be a good girl, and always be sure to be kind to your mother, for she has been very kind to us; and one more thing I have to beg of you, not to give your mind to dress, it is a very great snare; and to avoid the dancing room, it is often the first step toward the ruin of young women'*.

About five weeks before her death her mother inquired of her if she wished to be released from her suffering, and to be with her heavenly Father; her reply was, *'I have no wish of my own – I wish only what God pleases.'* Her mother said, 'My dear Patty, what shall I do when you are taken from me?' *'Oh, my dear mother, Christ is not dead, you must come and pour out your complaints to him, and he will not send you away empty.'* 'How often,' her mother states, 'has she wept to think what trouble she had given me; but she would say, *'Put your trust in God, and he will repay you for all your trouble.'*

The day before her death, she said to her mother, *'I believe my time will not be long with you, my dissolution is drawing nigh'*, and on being asked what were her feelings in the awful prospect, she said, *'All peace within – welcome death, sweet death to me. Glory be to God'*. In the evening of the same day several of her friends came to see her; she spoke little, but gave them to understand that she was willing to depart and be with Christ. Her mother thus describes the closing scene. 'About five in the morning she wished to be raised up in bed. I could not lift her. She said *'Let John* (her brother) *do it'* and said to him *'Come my dear, it will be the last time'*. He said, 'My dear Patty, you are very ill.' She said, *'Yes, my dear, but it will soon be over'*. She then lay still for some time, her brother and sister leaning over her, weeping very much. About half past ten I spoke to her, but we found that she could not speak. I said 'My dear, if it is all well, and all peace, open your eyes,' so she opened her eyes, looked up and smiled twice, and then her happy spirit took its flight about eleven o'clock in the forenoon of the 10th October 1837, aged 33 years and 8 months.

Chapter 3

Telling it How it Was

The Children Interviewed for the 1842 Royal Commission Examining Employment Conditions at the Mines of West Devon and Cornwall

In 1841, after pressure from Lord Ashley (later to become Lord Shaftesbury), four commissioners were appointed by parliament to investigate the conditions under which children and young people were working, at the various mines of the realm. They were instructed to report back in 1842. A sub-commissioner, who was believed to have good working knowledge of the industry, was identified for each major mining area, and was charged with the responsibility of gathering information and evidence. The person appointed to this task for the metalliferous mines of the South West was Charles Barham, Esq.

Born in Truro in 1804, Charles Barham had read medicine at Cambridge and had returned to Cornwall to practise, by 1837. It seems that much of his work was as a mine surgeon, and he had presented a paper entitled 'Some Remarks on the Diseases of Miners' to the Royal Institution of Cornwall, in November 1840. In his report to the Commissioners he had gathered information on the mines of Cornwall, the east bank of the Tamar and a few of the mines on Dartmoor. (He did not include those of the Teign Valley, Coombe Martin, the northern Dartmoor fringe or the Mendips).

Out of his concern for all mine employees, Barham stepped beyond his brief, and in his lengthy report included evidence on the working environment of adults, as well as the children and young people. In his appendix, he recorded summaries of 115 interviews which he conducted during 1841, of which 38 were with surface workers under the age of 18 years (18 boys and 20 girls). These are reproduced here, along with one interview with a woman who had been working at the mines for over 30 years, and all were from Cornwall. These summaries appear to be notes made during medical consultations, and are often a mixture of third person observation, and quoted speech. They do not appear to have been edited into a coherent piece of reportage, nor is there consistent gathering of information. However as a whole, they give a unique and valuable insight into the work, home-life and health of the young people who worked at surface in Cornwall, in the mid-19th century.

* * * * * * * * * * * * * * * * *

These interviews are set out as in the original report, using Barham's numbering system, but with some rationalisation of the punctuation. Notes of clarification, or general observations recorded by Barham (such a comments on general health, or ability to read and write) are retained in parenthesis. Where it has been possible to discover additional information about the subject of the interview, this has been added in the footnotes.

* * * * * * * * * * * * * * * * *

**No. 2. John Henry Martin, 12 years and 8 months old.
Examined at Trethellan, March 6th 1841.[1]**

I had gatherings when I was six months old (scrofulous affection of the right hip joint).

My father died two years ago. I can 'travel' and play with other boys. I don't feel any more in that leg than in the other. This is the first place I came to work, about a year and a half ago. I then went underground in Wheal Brewer (a mine at that time connected to this). My work was blowing air. This was 60 fathoms below adit, 120 fathoms from the surface, I climb 'tolerable well'. My work here is washing up. My feet are wet all day but I do not take cold. I have lost no time through sickness. I come here at 7 o'clock in the morning, take my dinner which I bring with me, at twelve. I generally done of potato pasty [sic].

---

[1] Possibly the son of copper miner William and Ann Martin of Tresavean (1841 Census Stithians 27/6/27)

He lives a mile off (in fact nearly two miles). Sometimes he travels the distance in half an hour. He has hot tea for breakfast with bread (barley or white) and treacle. His mother has 12 children, eight boys and four girls. Three brothers older than himself work underground here, and one sister at Tresavean. Mother keeps a little farm in which the younger brother assists and the elder ones too when out of 'core' (course or turn of work at the mine).

I go to Sunday School at the Methodist Chapel at Stithians and have gone there for three or four years. I learn to read. [I heard him read in the New Testament which he did tolerably well].

I have no holidays except Christmas Day and Good Friday. I change when I get home if my clothes are wet. I get potatoes boiled or baked for supper and go to bed at seven or soon after. I get 12s. a month wages, from which 2d. is taken for the doctor (for surgical assistance only). I earned 10s. last month. The cold weather prevented me from working some days. I came to the floors and found the tables covered with snow and the pickers could not work. I went home again. None of the boys complain of being tired. I give my wages to my mother.

**No. 3. Samuel Tippet, 10 years and 7 months old.
Examined Trethellan, March 6th 1841.**

He has worked here at the floors a fortnight now. He worked before at the mine for two spurs, two months each time, at the slimes. He gave up because 'the slimes was 'knacked.' He is now washing up. He lives with his grandfather about half a mile off. He pays his wages to his grandfather. He had seven shillings per month on his first spur and now he gets ten. He sometimes feels tired when he leaves work, chiefly in the back and legs. He brings potato 'hobban' with him for dinner. For breakfast he gets milk and water and bread, barley and wheat mixed. For supper baked potatoes, with pork sometimes. He goes to bed at eight, but likes to stay up longer. He goes to New Church (Lanner) and has been to Sunday School two years, where he learns to read and spell. [Heard him read in the Testament and he read pretty well].

**No. 4. William Harris, 15 years old.
Examined at Trethellan, March 6th 1841.**

He is quite well in health. He has been at work four or five years. He was at Tresavean first. He had been here only for ten months, riddling or wheeling stuff. He feels tired at night in the 'chines' (loins). This passes off with rest. The only accident he has suffered from was a gathering of the finger from it being poisoned with the 'mundic water'. This kept him off work for a week. He feels nothing from it now. His father died from a hurt 12 years ago, his mother was left with five children. She has married again. His father-in-law takes good care of him. He is 'hind' with Mr. Jenkins (a gentleman living in the country, some miles of). He goes to Sunday School sometimes but he has never been at any other. His wages are 15s. a month, which he pays to his mother. All the family are employed in mining, they are all healthy. He works sometimes a little at harrowing and different things about the farm after he comes home from the mine, but he is not forced to do so.

No. 5. Thomas Knuckey Martin, 14 years and 2 months old.
Examined at Trethellan, March 6th 1841.

He has a slight hoarseness and has had it 'to and again just ever since last Christmas.' [sic] He work is jigging. He sometimes gets wet in the feet at work. He does not feel the cold. He does not change his shoes and stockings when he gets home. He does not always get them dried at night for him to go out on the next morning. He lives with his grandmother, his mother lives at some distance. He gets a potato hobban for dinner, barley bread and butter for breakfast and boiled potatoes with fish at times for supper. He has worked in this mine for three years, and at Tresavean two years before. He went to day school for two years before going to Tresavean and since that to Sunday School at a Methodist Chapel. [On trial he wrote fairly, ciphered a little and read well].

No. 6. Grace Bowden, 17 years and 9 months old.
Examined at Trethellan, March 6th 1841.

She has been in good health at the mine, where she has worked for a year and seven months. She was previously employed at straw bonnet making for two years. She gave this up in consequence of her failing health. She finds that her employment at the mine agrees with her very well. Her work is spalling and cobbing. She would as soon do one as the other.

She lives two miles off, in lodgings. For these she pays 6d. a week which includes cooking her victuals. She is not very comfortable in this. She brings a pasty for lunch. She earns 9d per day. She went to Sunday School in Lanner. [She reads pretty well. I was informed that she was expecting to be married 'ere long].

Cobbing   Jigging

Washing and Picking

Bucking and Sieving

Fig. 6 Some Copper Dressing Tasks c. 1858

James Henderson

Spalling

Packing   Tozing

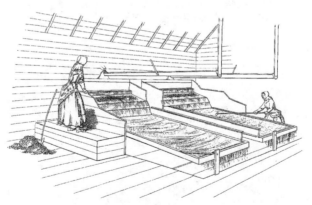

Racking

Fig. 7 Some Tin Dressing Tasks c. 1858

James Henderson

No. 7. Martha Williams, 11 years and 5 months old.
Examined at Trethellan March 6th 1841.[2]

She was very well and hearty. She is employed picking which she finds easy work. She has been a year at work here. This was the first place she went to work. She lived at home before with her widowed mother in Redruth, and does so still. Her mother takes in washing. Her father has been dead this brave while. He died when she was about two years old. She went to day school before she came to the mine and learned to read and write. She goes now to the Baptist Sunday School. [I put her to read in the Testament and she read very badly].

She walks out from Redruth in the morning and back in the evening (a distance of more than five miles a day). She gets milk and bread as much as she can eat, for breakfast, pasty with meat in it for lunch, and tea and potatoes for supper. She goes to bed about 7 pm.

No. 18. Mary Ann Roscorle, 12 years and 6 months.
Examined at Tresavean, March 23rd 1841.

She is employed at picking tables. About 30 to 40 children work together on the same floor with herself. She goes to work from her home at six in the morning and leaves at half past five. She takes part of what she brings with her for dinner at crowst at 10 in the morning, when a quarter of an hour is allowed. She never works the regular hour of leaving. She finds she has enough time to eat her dinner with comfort. She does not suffer from cold in the shed at dinner time. She has learned to read in the workhouse. Her mother was unable to provide for her. She therefore lives with a man called Reed, who boards and lodges her and to whom she pays when she gets. He treats her kindly.

No. 19. Jane Uren, 16 years old.
Examined at Tresavean, March 23rd 1841.[3]

How old are you? 'Sixteen'.
How do you know your age? 'I have always known it'.

---

[2] Possibly the daughter of charwoman Ann Williams (widowed) of South Downs Redruth, with two older brothers also working at a copper mine in 1841 (1841 Census Redruth 143/12/6/50)

[3] Possibly the daughter of Francis (mine carrier) and Sally Uren of Pennance, Gwennap (1841 Census Gwennap 137/10/43/40)

How many people work in the same place as yourself? 'I can't exactly tell'.

She had been cobbing and has been two or three months at this work. She has been working in these mines 'in the six years'. She lives a mile and a half off and very seldom works overtime.

Do you leave work before the regular hour of closing? 'I generally 'cob' a barrow and a half (the barrow is about 1½ cwt) and if this is done often go at five o'clock.'

What do you drink with your dinner? 'Water'.

She cannot read and has not gone to school lately. Her father has ten children. Five of them employed at the mines. The older ones can read the Bible.

No. 20. Mary Johns, 14 years and 6 months old.
Examined at Tresavean, March 23rd 1841.

She is employed at spalling and carrying, the latter is the hardest work. She has worked here for about a year. She was in service before. She found it hard work at first, but her health has been better than when in service. She lives at Redruth two miles distant. She feels the work heavy. She suffers from a pain in the back and side, the latter increasing, particularly when carrying. She had a pain in the side before she came to the mine, chiefly when sitting. It comes on now about 11 or 12 but passes off with further work. She works out in all weathers, and gets wet at times; but does not often take cold. She was in day school in Redruth, and still goes to Sunday School. [Heard her read which she did tolerably.]

No. 21. Elizabeth Larkeek, 18 years old.
Examined at Tresavean, March 23rd 1841.

She lives in Redruth. Her work is bucking. She has been five months here and two and a half years at other mines. She does not feel much fatigue, except a pain in the left arm at the change of weather, which she imputes to a sudden strain lifting too heavy a weight. She does not know any accidents having happened in the mines from carrying or other work at the surface. She is now obliged to buck eight barrows for a shilling. Some months ago the same price was paid for six barrows. When she has earned that sum she usually goes home, often about four o'clock. She went to work first at 14 years 6 months, and before that she went to day school where she learned sewing. She still goes to Sunday School. [Found that she could read tolerably.]

No. 22. Richard Uren, 11 years 6 months.
Examined at Tresavean, March 23rd 1841

His mother told him his age. He had been at work two years. His work is washing up. He lives near the mine. He does not complain of anything. He has no father, he died of 'a galloping consumption' years ago. [Heard him read which he did tolerably.]

No. 23. Joseph Odgers Vincent, 14 years and 6 months old.
Examined at Tresavean, March 23rd 1841.

His work is jigging and he had been two years at this and altogether three years at work. He finds his work causes him pain in the chines, and hears most of the boys complain of this after working nine hours. He generally gets his feet wet, but does not take cold. He lives two miles off. Twice or sometimes three times a week he gets away about two o'clock, having finished his task. He will soon go riddling. He was four years at John Martin's school at Stythians [sic] and since has been at Sunday School. [He reads tolerably well.]

No. 28. Eliza Allen, 20 years old.
Examined at Truro, March 10th 1841.

She has been at Consols two years and is employed sitting down cobbing. She worked with her father before. She suffered from shortness of breath, and felt her legs go weak, so that she could hardly stand on them from the first. Her wages are 18s. a month, but she could not earn half that sum. She finds it difficult to keep her feet dry and always catches cold when she does not. She never went to school but can scarcely read at all. She can sew a little for her mother. [She is rather a delicately constitutioned girl and is now labouring under disorder of the system, for which she seeks my advice.]

No. 32. Anna Wasley, 20 years old.
Examined at Truro March 10th 1841.

She works at Cakes & Ale Mine. She went to work at 13 and suffers from shortness of breath on any exertion and has done so for the last twelve months. She works ten hours a day, from seven to half past five, with half an hour for dinner and has done so from the first. Her mother has seven children, five boys and two girls. They have gone to work at seven or eight years old.

No. 33. Sally Fall, 19 years old.
Examined at Truro March 10th 1841.[4]

She suffers from pain in the left side, palpitation and shortness of breath. She has worked among the Gwennap Mines. She has of late years been chiefly employed bucking. She considers she overstrained herself last Whitsuntide in lifting a heavy weight. She went to work at 11 and did not feel it hard till she was laid up with inflammation in her side when about 13 years of age. She did not go to school and can hardly read. Her mother has six children, one is a boy of 17 and he works at Tresavean underground. He went underground about nine years old. Their father died of cancer. His death obliged them to go to work early. He reads tolerably in the Bible and enjoys good health. His mother is afraid his slight living might injure him as he grows fast. A younger boy which is about 10 has worked at the stamping mills for about twelve months and has not suffered. The other children are younger. [Stout and florid but constitutionally disordered.]

No. 45. Eliza Evans, 17 years old.
Examined at Truro, March 24th 1841.[5]

She has gone to the mines from time to time, but found even picking too hard for her. The stooping hurts her head and she suffers from headaches. Her mother has six children. One girl is older than her and is employed at Budnick racking. One boy of 15 works underground. [Delicate.]

---

[4] Possibly the daughter of widow Catherine Faull (44 yrs) of Tresoddern, Gwennap, and a patient in Truro Infirmary by 6th June 1841 (1841 Census Gwennap 137/12/39/15, Truro 147/20/1)

[5] Possibly the daughter of Edmund + Eliza Evans of Landrona, Perranzabuloe, with a younger brother working at tin mine in 1841 (1841 Census Perranzabuloe 150/18/35/12)

No. 46. Fanny Francis, 17 years old.
Examined Truro March 24th 1841.[6]

She works in the United Mines and suffers from dyspepsia and has an eruption on the skin. She has worked at the mines about six years and always enjoyed good health till she fell in carrying, about three months since when she had fits. She went to day schooling before she worked at the mine, and has since attended Sunday School. She now acts as teacher once in three weeks at the Bryanite Chapel. Her mother, Martha Francis is 50 years old and is a widow and has five children, all miners. She put the eldest son underground at 12 and the second at fifteen. They did not complain about their work. All of them went to school but poor people cannot do all they would.

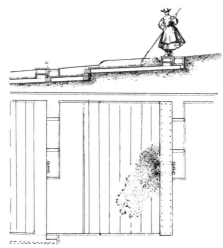

Fig. 8 Buddle as used at Frongoch Lead Mine
from Robert Hunt, 'British Mining' 1884

No. 47. Jane Sandow, 17 years and 6 months old.
Examined at Truro March 24th 1841.

She suffers from gastrodynia. She works at Wheal Gorland. She has three miles to walk to the mine. She is generally employed cobbing. Her mother has ten children, all girls but one. The elder ones are employed at the mines. They generally go about ten years old. All go to school, chiefly Sunday School. They learn to sew and knit a little at dame school.

---

[6] Probably the daughter of Paul + Martha Francis, of Tippets Stamps, Kea (1841 Census Kea 147/11/17/70)

No. 52. Thomas Fidock, 13 years old.
Examined at East Wheal Crofty March 26th 1841.

He is employed buddling. He first went to work at Stray Park, at 9 years of age. He comes to work at 7 and goes at 5. He has task work once a month perhaps. He went to day school before going to work at the mines, and since that has attended Sunday School at Penponds (Wesleyan Methodist). [I heard him read in the Testament and he read well but could not explain the meaning of the word multitude nor say how many apostles there were.]

No. 53. John Richards, 13 years old.
Examined at East Wheal Crofty March 26th 1841.

He has been here for three years and is employed buddling. It is easy work. He gets up at half past five in the morning. He has a task set him about once a fortnight and can then leave work about two. [This boy wrote a little and read well. I also gave him some arithmetical questions which he calculated mentally very well.]

No. 57. Michael Loam Allen Nicholls, 11 years and 6 months old.
Examined at Truro, March 31st 1841.

He is employed as an engine boy at the United Mines. He has been there these eight months. He received a blow from the handle of the engine, while brushing out the place. Boys are not usually employed as young about the engine.

No. 58. William Bennett, 11 years and 6 months old.
Examined at Truro, March 31st 1841.

He works at Wheal Kitty in St. Agnes in the 12 fathom level. He went underground when 11 years old in Polgooth and worked at the 30 fathom level. He was chiefly employed in wheeling stuff (rolling).

He had good health and was employed watching stamps in which he was exposed to the wet being 13 hours at night from five in the evening to seven on the following morning, two weeks out of three, thus engaged. Taking it in turns with a comrade to watch and lying down about the boilers or some warm place to sleep, every three or six hours. But he did not suffer from this.

No. 60. Christina Morom, 53 years old.
Examined at Truro March 31st 1841.

She first went to work at about 10 years old in the Gwennap mines. She did not suffer much until about 20 years ago when she was seized with lumbago which she imputed to the hardness of the work. She has been affected with this and other pains more or less ever since.

No. 61. Jane Jewell, 21 years old.
Examined at Truro March 10th 1841.

She has worked a fortnight at Consols but found she could not continue. She has always found that the 'bal' (mine) disagreed with her which she attributes chiefly to the mundic water. The smell made her sick when the water was warm. Her father is a miner at Consols and is in a declining state, and is about 50 years of age.

No. 63. Charles Manuel, 16 years and 6 months.
Examined at Carnon, March 30th 1841.

He had been here about five years. After being two years at surface work, which he went underground did not suffer from the work at grass [sic]. Underground he was employed rolling (wheel barrows). He soon began to feel pain in his breasts, which he attributes chiefly to the damp. He continued to work for nearly two years, when he was obliged to be put into the hands of the doctor. He was then ill for three weeks. After this he returned to work, but was obliged to give up again in a week and was confined a fortnight. After this he worked at the surface only, and has scarcely lost any time since. When working underground he was forced to go up into the end of the level for the stuff, when he drew in poor air. Afterwards he would spit black stuff. Many of his companions did so. He met with one accident from the falling of a stone from the side of the level on his arm. He only worked overtime three times whilst he was underground. Other boys did so more frequently. He knew of a boy working five double stems out of six days last week.

He was going to an evening school during the winter months and paid 3d. a week. He learnt reading and writing. The Bible and Testament were the books used. No instruction by questioning was given. He did not find that he was tired by his work so as not to attend his schooling. He went to school at half past six and stayed until half past eight. He got to bed about ten. He gives his wages to his father. [Reads pretty well.]

No. 86. Martha Buckingham, 14 years and 1 month old.
Examined at the Consolidated Mines, May 5th 1841.[7]

She has been at work for about four years She has been employed 'picking' all the time, except 'carrying' now and then, and 'griddling' or 'spalling' once in a way to help the pair when they are busy. 'Carrying' is the hardest work. This gives her pain in her back sometimes and now and then she does this for the whole day. She gets wet in winter, the wind and rain coming under the shed. She catches cold sometimes, most of the girls do. She has been at home a fortnight by cold, caught chiefly by getting her feet wet in coming and going. The girls cannot get a pair of shoes to change when they come to the mine. It is hard enough to get one pair to wear. She also 'overheated her blood' by carrying and working hard and has had a breaking out since. She usually comes to work at seven in the morning, and goes home at half past five, but at sampling, which occurs about once a month, they come at six and stay till eight. They do this for a week, sometimes a fortnight. This is the case now. She lives at Bissow [sic] Bridge (three miles distant). She gets supper after she gets home and goes to bed as soon as she can, at half past nine or ten. She gets up at four. There are seven in her family. She has no father, he died in Scotland about eight years ago, and he was a miner. All are older than her except one. All work to the mines, except the youngest. One brother is ill. He is working at Poldice in a hot place and then had to fill the kibble in cold water. She gets her breakfast before leaving in the morning. No time is allowed for crowst (lunch) but at nine or ten they take a bit of pasty when the agent is not looking, holding it with one hand and working with the other. When they work overtime they are allowed to stay at home a day when sampling is over. They are not paid anything more than their regular wages. There is not regular work for all in the summer but in the winter they all come, or nearly all. They are allowed half an hour for dinner. They warm their pasties and hobbans at the dry when the weather is cold. They take their dinners under a shed, the girls all together. An anker (small barrel) of cold water is brought for them to drink. No water is to be had except a long way off. She feels very tired to walk home. No tasks are given. They always work to half past five. When they work late on the other days they leave work at half past five on Saturdays. She goes to Sunday School with the Methodists and learns to read and spell with the Catechism. [She read pretty well. Has a cough and a papulous eruption but has the appearance of being generally healthy.]

---

[7] Probably the daughter of widow Delia Buckingham of Bissoe (1841 Census Gwennap 147/9/1/31)

No. 87. Mary Verran, 14 years and 10 months old.
Examined at the Consolidated Mines, May 15th 1841.

She had been working here four years, always here. Her employment has been picking. Carrying and other work at sampling time just every day. She feels pains in the back and side chiefly about the middle part of the day. She feels it after she lays down at night. She lives about a mile off and gets up about half past four or five o'clock. Her father was a miner but now goes with the tram wagons on the railway. The wages are better than at the mines. She hears most of the girls complain of pain in the back from carrying. They do not complain much except of the carrying. She finds half an hour rather short for dinner. They were allowed half a day for Whitsuntide, two hours at Midsummer and two hours on Christmas Eve and all Christmas Day and Good Friday. The girls bring hobbans, plum and potato, more than pasties. Not many bring bread and butter. A hobban is not as good as a pasty. Some are and made with barley. She gets fish for supper and potatoes, sometimes a stew, roast potatoes or broth. Sometimes, but very seldom, the girls are obliged to give up their work, from being faint or sick. Two or three months ago three or four girls, were obliged to be led home. They were employed at out door work, griddling or spalling. She went to day school before she came to work and goes to Sunday School twice in the day. [She reads pretty well. Thought John the Baptist had written the Gospel. Had never heard of the Sadducees. She is rather robust in her appearance.]

No. 88. Elizabeth Curnow, 24 years old.
Examined at the Consolidated Mines, May 15th 1841.

She has been about eight years coming into the mines. She has only worked these last two days for two months. She is taken with a gradual loss of strength and appetite once or twice a year and finds the harder she works the less she can eat. Sometimes she comes to the mines and sometimes she goes into service when her health is more established. She does not find much difference as to her health between these occupations. The work is harder for the time but when one leaves work there is nothing more to do. She comes at seven in the morning and stays till eight in the evening at sampling. This is once a month and lasts about a week or fortnight, more often a fortnight. She is generally employed cobbing. They are paid by the barrow, for six barrows. The half hour is not long enough for dinner, especially for those who have bad teeth. They can always warm their dinners if they like. She lives about two miles off from the mine. She gets very cold about the legs with the broken stones in winter and the house runs with water. Most complain of it. The older girls generally have pasties. [Rather sallow complexion.]

No. 89. Christian Pascoe, 17 years 4 months old.
Examined at the Consolidated Mines, May 15th 1841.

She has come to work about five years or rather more. She has always been at these mines. She was employed for two years picking, then she went to the floors spalling and carrying and she had now been cobbing for seven months. This work is not so trying to the body as working out of doors. She was let in because she was not able to continue to work out. She had pains in her back and was falling into decline by it, her breath getting very short, till she took medicine for it. The feet get wet with water coming in and the stones are wet when there is rain. She can 'cobbie' six barrows a day for which she is paid 8d. That is all they are allowed to get when they do not stay until eight. She could not do more well, the work is very hard. She can cobbbie a barrow and sometimes two in the overtime. She still has a shortness of breath at all times and pain in the back after working a good many hours. She lives one mile off. She gets up at six and does not go to bed until 10 or 11. Her mother, being a widow, and there being household [duties?] and needlework to be done after she gets home. Her father was hurt in the mine (Wood Mine) and brought up blood and fell into a consumption and died eight months ago. [Complexion indicating venous congestion.]

No. 90. William Trethewy, 13 years old.
Examined at the Consolidated Mines, May 15th 1841

He had been working three or four years at the mine. He has been rolling or jigging. He worked underground for a month or two, at the 110 fathom level and was employed turning the borer. He was very well then. He caught a cold a few days ago when he stayed up all night jigging. This was the only time he had worked at night. It was fine weather but all the boys caught a cold, ten of them. He had very good health generally. He stays for six to about eight about a week or fortnight in the month. He feels his arms and legs pain him sometimes but it is as well as ever after he gets into bed. They are allowed a day or so over their regular pay for this extra work. They take a bit of something about 10 o'clock in the morning. There is no regular time allowed. He got on well climbing when he was underground and would be glad to go down again if he could. He felt nothing from the powder smoke or poor air. He did not spit black stuff. Rolling is the hardest work at the surface and jigging in a sieve. Only two of the boys, myself and another can do it. There are only two boys older than myself on the floors. He never went to day school except when a little boy. He goes to Sunday School at St Day where he began to learn to read and write a week ago. He lives in St Day (one mile distant). Generally he brings a potato hobban for dinner. His wages are 12s. a month. [He reads fairly well. He is now hoarse from catarrh but he is a fine boy.]

No. 91. Elisha Morcom, 13 years 6 months old.
Examined at the Consolidated Mines, May 14th 1841.

He has been home for today and for two days in consequence of having received a blow in the bowels from a stone which a boy threw at him wantonly. He has been ill from time to time with pain in the bowels, sides, etc., he has been kept at home by sickness a month or two in four years. His general work is jigging. He has been rolling this afternoon. He has been working at grass four years and a half, always in the same mine with the exception of two or three months. His wages are 10s 6d a month. He lives two miles off. Generally, he gets up at four o'clock or soon after. He brings a potato hoggan for dinner mostly. Generally, not always, he leaves work at half past five on Saturdays. and would get up at 4 am. He went to day school and learnt to read and to write a little. [Reads tolerably.]

No. 92. Richard Jeffrey, 9 years and 1 month old.
Examined at the Consolidated Mines, May 14th 1841

He belongs to the boxes (picking tables) and he gets 6s a month. He has been eight months here. He has had very good health. His hands get sore, especially when he is long at the shambles (the heaps to which the stones rejected by the pickers are taken). He stays till eight o'clock now. He is tired with his days work. He lives two and a half miles away. His father died out in Mexico of the cholera. His mother was left with four, three girls and himself. He is the youngest. He does not go to school. He has never gone yet. Two of his sisters work at this mine, the other a dressmaker. He cannot read.

No. 101. Harry Thomas, 10 years 11 months old.
Examined at the Charlestown Mines, April 1st 1841.

He has been here 12 days. He is employed tending the buddle, and finds it rather hard as yet. He was at day school but goes to Sunday School. [Healthy boy. He reads very badly. Cannot write.]

Fig. 9 Round Buddle at what is believed to be Silverbrook Lead Mine, Ilsington c. 1858
courtesy of Torquay Museum

No. 102. William Rowett, 13 years old.
Examined at the Charlestown Mines, April 1st 1841.[8]

He has been four years in the mine. He has always been employed tending the buddle. Another boy of his own age works with him. He comes to the mine at seven in the morning, and leaves work at half past five in the evening.

How often do you work after half past five? 'Once or twice a month we work as long as we can see and then go to supper. We are allowed an hour to supper, then we work by candlelight till 12 and we are allowed till one and eat some pasty but do not go home. After this we work till two in the afternoon. I am paid for this by the day and a half. I put this into my own pocket. Sometimes I feel sleepy, sometimes very well.'

---

[8] Possibly son of tin miner Charles + Ann Rowett of Boscoppa Downs (1841 Census St Austell 146/4/8/8)

His father is a timberman in the mine. He has nine children, eight boys and one girl, six of them are at this mine with his father. He was at day school for a year and a half before he came to the mine and then to Sunday School until a year and a half ago (at Mount Charles Wesleyan Meeting) but he has forgotten what he learnt. He works with his father after he leaves the mine. He does not feel tired. He has been quite well.

No. 103. Elizabeth Hocking, 17 years 6 months.
Examined at the Charlestown Mines, April 1st 1841.

Her work is spalling. She has been here four years. She had been spalling for three years and recking before. She found the spalling much the harder work and still finds it hard. She feels pain in her limbs, sometimes in her back. She does not always get rid of it on lying down. She stays up till nine or ten and gets up at half past five. She works an hour or an hour and a half overtime about once a month. She gives her mother all her wages, and what she can of extra pay. [A strong ruddy girl.]

No. 104. Elizabeth Davey, 17 years old.
Examined at the Charlestown Mines, April 1st 1841.

She has been here a year and a half and is employed at the recking. She was in service before she came to the mine. She finds this employment agrees with her better than service but is liable to take cold. [Has a good colour but looks rather delicate.]

No. 109. William Cullis, 17 years old.
Examined at Fowey Consols mines, April 2nd 1841.

He is employed jigging on the floors. He worked before at the crushers (grinder) but found it disagreed with his stomach. He was laid up three times and found his breath short. He lost his appetite and brought up 'old black trade'. He hears other boys complain of this sometimes. He found his back aches sometimes. When at the grinder he used to work sometimes (four times in six months) day and night from seven in the evening to five the next morning. He has been healthy at the other work. He went to day school for two years and learnt to write a little but has forgotten it. He went to Sunday School, Tywardreath Church School, till about a year ago, but only learnt reading and spelling. [Reads pretty well.]

No. 111. John Spargoe, 11 years and 4 months old.
Examined at Fowey Consols mines, April 2nd 1841.

He had been two years in this mine and is employed jigging. He finds his back only aches a little but can play afterwards. He has a task once or twice a week and can get away at two or three o'clock. He works for himself afterwards when he can. He had never works at night. He went to day school about a year before he came here. He can read in the Testament. He goes to Sunday School. [Reads badly. A healthy boy.]

No. 112. Mary Buller, 15 years and 10 months old.
Examined at Fowey Consols mines, April 2nd 1841.

She has been working here for about six years, generally spalling and cobbing. She has generally good health. She does not feel the work. She leaves at five in the evening, and never stays later, except last month. Perhaps once a week she had a task and can get away at three or half past three. 'Most of the girls who I know of and I know a pretty deal of them in the mines are strong and hearty'. "One of them' (whose name she mentioned) 'is terribly weakly and looks very earthy, though she is 18.' She went to a day school for three years and learnt to read and sew and knit. She has forgotten her reading. She has not had clothes to go to Sunday School. Her mother is a widow and could not afford to keep them at school.

No. 113. Caroline Coom, 11 years old.
Examined at Fowey Consols mines, April 2nd 1841.

She has been working here for two years, and is employed in picking. She finds it easy and pleasant and does not feel tired at the end of the day. None of the girls picking complain of anything. They get cold sometimes. She has no tasks and does not leave before five. She has had a fever since she has been working at the mine. She does not know how long. She goes to Sunday School and reads the Testament there. [Reads a little.]

Bibliography

BBP 1842 (Charles Barham) *The Royal Commission for Inquiring into the Employment and Condition of Children and Young Persons in the Mines of Cornwall and Devonshire*

Chapter 4

A Miscellany of Surface Captains

While there are a few surviving firsthand accounts from the women and children who worked at the mines, there is also another category of surface workers who also, on occasion, left records of their experiences. These are the male labourers, and men in positions of minor authority or leadership. It is their memories which are shared here.

Miners could rarely work underground beyond the age of forty, and many were unable to continue at an even younger age. The damage to lungs and heart meant that they could no longer climb the fathoms of ladders back to surface at the end of the day. If these ailing miners were well enough, the mine agents would try to find them work at surface. The less experienced might become surface labourers (wheeling barrows or 'ragging' rock). If they were strong enough they might be employed as kibble landers (a very dangerous job, also requiring much skill). Those with longer service might be found tasks with more responsibility, such as being in charge of the Miners' Dry. For the most senior, a place might be found as a Surface Captain. While in later years, Surface Captains were employed directly by the mine adventurers, in earlier years, they may often have been subcontracted. They would agree to dress a particular amount of ore, at a pre-set price per ton of mineral produced, ready for smelting. In both cases, the Surface Captain would be responsible for recruiting the surface workers under him, and would supervise their tasks. He would also be responsible for the safe and efficient running of the dressing equipment. If subcontracted, he would then have to pay his workers out of his takings.

The first accounts reproduced here, come from Billy Bray (who worked at surface in at least two different capacities; as a 'captain-dresser' and surface labourer). These are followed by interviews with four Surface Captains and the manager of a Men's Dry, conducted for the 1842 Royal Commission. Finally there are short anecdotes from Captain Benjamin Bennetts, who managed a tin stream on the Red River, and John Jenkin's detailed account of work on the dressing floors and sawmill house at Delabole Slate Quarry, both probably from the last quarter of the 19th century.

* * * * * * * * * * * * * * * *

Billy Bray, Captain-Dresser

Fig. 10 Portrait of Billy Bray
Courtesy of the Billy Bray memorial Trust

One of Cornwall's most well-known and certainly most eccentric preachers was Billy Bray (1794-1868). Born in the Twelveheads area of Gwennap, he became a Bible Christian (Bryanite) preacher and was also involved in 'church planting'. Despite personal poverty, he inspired others to help him build three new chapels in the area, between 1830 and 1838. A miner all his working life, he worked initially at the local copper mines, but then at Wheal Friendship (in Devon) for about seven years, and probably for a similar length of time in the St Neot and St Blazey areas. Three stories of his experiences at the dressing floors are transcribed here. Each are recounted by Billy to illustrate his understanding of God's providence, and it is in that context we read them. Two are drawn from his journal (which Billy began writing in 1864)[1] and the third from his biography, written by Frederick Bourne.

* * * * * * * * * * * * * * * *

In the early days after Billy's conversion, he found himself in difficulty because he was expected to work on Sundays. In part of his journal he recalls how, after a breach through to flooded old workings in the Cusvey and Wheal Fortune part of the Great Consols mine, the only way to keep the levels clear of water was to keep pumping. As a result, one of Billy's

---

[1] The Journal, written in Billy's hand, is very difficult to decipher. Chris Wright in his book *Billy Bray in His Own Words* has painstakingly transcribed the script, attempting to clarify its meaning while retaining Billy's patterns of speech.

duties as a member of his tutwork team was to 'draw water' on the Sabbath. (This task would require him to work at surface at the horse whim, and land the kibbles of water as they were drawn up from the mine). His non-appearance for that work on the Sunday he was rostered resulted in his instant dismissal. After a kindly intervention by the mine purser [2] he was temporarily given employment at surface, carting ashes from the engine house. This did not need to be done on a Sunday.

*'The water was drawn to the surface by a horse whim, every twelve hours, and one of us men used to land it. It was drawn up Saturday nights at six o'clock, at Sunday mornings at 6 o'clock and in the evening at six o'clock. One Sunday in eight it was my core to land water. On the day it was my Sunday to the land the water I was at Hicks Mill Chapel...
[and] I stayed there that Sunday and let the water go down to the bottom of the shaft, and it did not hinder no one.*

On the Monday morning I went to the mine at 6 o'clock to land water... I met Captain Hosken coming out and he said to me, "Where wast thee yesterday, that thee wast not here landing water?" I said to him, "It was not the Lord's will that I should come." He said, "I'll Lord's will thee. Thou shalt not work here any more."

...Then William Roberts, my comrade that worked with me, said. "Captain Hosken hast turned me away too, and you know that is not my fault."

I said "No, you shall not be turned away, for it is my fault, not yours. I will go to him and tell him."

I said to the captain, "You must not turn away William Roberts, for it was not his fault. It was my core to land the water, not his."

*...The clerk that was in the counting house, he was called Mister Mitchel, said "If I feel like William Bray do, I would not work Sunday neither."
...Then the captain said "Thee should go to work if thou wants."*

I said to him, "That is no good, for shall I not work Sundays? Have you any place else to put me to work?"

He said, "Thee may go down to the engine and wheel away the ashes from the engine if you will."

---

[2] Mine clerk and accountant.

I was glad when he said so, for I could go to meetings or preaching every night. If I was working underground I could not, for us work underground some cores by night.

So I took my wheelbarrow and went to the engine and wheeled away the ashes, and they that seed I told them what the Lord had done for me."

* * * * * * * * * * * * * * *

Also transcribed here are two stories from when Billy was a 'captain-dresser'. The first account (from his journal), about a whirlwind threatening the dressing floor, took place at Wheal Sisters in St Neot in either 1847 or 1848.

'When I was at St Neot, at a mine called Wheal Sisters, I was what they called a dressing captain that looked to the boys and maidens, to keep them to work. One day when we was at the mine we saw in the distance a whirlwind. It appeared to us to be from twelve to fifteen feet wide.

You might say that you could not see the wind. True, we could not see the wind, but we could see the effects, for it was tearing the bushes out of the hedges. There was a shaft they was sinking a little time before, but as it happened the shaft men was not there. And thanks be to God they was not, for there was a timber house over the shaft.

The whirlwind threw down the house that was over the shaft, and the shaft was not far from we. The wind had a great power. There was as much as fifty boys and maidens with me, and the whirlwind seemed to be coming in a right line unto us. When the boys and maidens saw that, they fell down on their knees and cried to the Lord to have mercy on them. And the dear Lord heard them and had mercy on them, for he turned the whirlwind another way around the barrow.

After it left where we was, it over-seat a farmers cart house….There was a great deal of timber where we was. There was timber around the shaft and iron too, and the bucking house and the cobbing house. So had not the dear Lord turned the whirlwind, it was looking as though that whirlwind would throw down the great part of it.

But as I said before, when the boys and girls fell down on their knees and cried for mercy, the dear Lord had mercy on them….for there was many converted at that time. Among them was two little boys about twelve years of age. One of them, John Hicks, is now a preacher and has been for some years.'

This second account (from Bourne's biography) describes a particular tender taken up by Billy, as Surface Captain, for dressing copper ore. It is not clear at which mine he was working, but the story illustrates the precarious nature of these agreements. The price, agreed beforehand, might underestimate the amount of mineral in the rock brought to surface, in which case the surface captain would be paid handsomely. More often, though, the ore would prove to be poorer than hoped, so the payment made for dressing would not cover the wages and costs.

'On one occasion, in his capacity as captain-dresser, he [Billy Bray] was engaged to dress a quantity of ore, and had to employ a number of young persons. But the general opinion was, that the lot was worthless, and for a time it was a great trial to Billy as there would be nothing for him, and worse still, nothing for those under him. "*Why, the people will say, there's that ould Billy Bray, and ould Bryanite, an ould rogue, he hath cheated the boys and maidens of their wages. A pretty Christian he!*" But Billy wrestled and laboured in prayer … [and] to all suggestions, from whatever quarter they came, his answer was, "*I don't care whether the stuff is worth anything or not. The Lord has told me he will bring me through, and I believe him.*"….On the "sampling" day the "stuff" was to be found more valuable than any person expected, enabling Billy to pay the boys and girls their wages, his own, and then have £5 left for himself'.

Surface Captains & At the Dry

Interviews from the 1842 Royal Commission
Investigating the Employment Conditions at the Mines
of West Devon and Cornwall

While collecting evidence for the 1842 Royal Commission, in 1841, Charles Barham interviewed four Surface Captains. They were employed at very different mines, both in terms of geography and the mineral produced. They included the Carn Brea Copper Mines (in the central mining area), the Cornubian Lead Mine (on the north coast of Cornwall, in Perranzabuloe), and Balleswidden Tin and Levant Copper Mines (on the St Just peninsula). The ages of these Captains ranged from 30 to 44 years old. As with the interviews with the boys and girls, Charles Barham had no set format to the questions he asked. As a result, the interviews transcribed here give us a random mix of personal stories and working experience of these Surface Captains, along with descriptions of the working conditions of the young people they employed. A fifth interview from the Report is also included. It was with Charles Burnet, who was in charge of the Mens' Dry at West Wheal Jewell (a copper mine in St Day parish).

* * * * * * * * * * * * * * * * *

No. 40. Mr Richard Carpenter, 30 years old.
Examined at Redruth, March 20th 1841.[3]

He is employed at the Carn Brea Mines in overlooking a party dressing ores. He has been so engaged for five years during which he has never been kept from his work by illness, except one day. He has 30 under his charge of whom only two are girls. On the whole those under his eye have enjoyed good health but he considers that a great many suffer from want of sufficient nourishment. There is no way of punishing except by spaling, which is deducted as part of the day, in case of negligence. By way of reward they have a job given them to do which may be finished before the regular hour of leaving work.

No. 84. The Captain of Dressers.
Examined at the Cornubian Lead Mines, April 27th 1841.

The boys at the surface had been very badly behaved when he came there twelve month since. They were constantly pelting and splashing each other and hooting passers by. He told them he would discharge the first offender and it was soon put a stop to. They have become very much more quiet of late and for the last three months they have held a meeting at dinner time among themselves, at which they sing hymns and have prayers. Five of them also met for mutual instruction in the chapel in the evenings on which it is not used for worship. Two young men are talking of teaching writing gratuitously. They mostly go three miles to their

---

[3] Probably Richard Carpenter, tin ore dresser of Carn Brea (1841 Census Illogan 142/2/27/8)

house. They would be glad to avail themselves of an evening school were there was one within reach.

The surface boys and girls are allowed 10 minutes for crowst at 10 o'clock. The girls are very well behaved. He thinks the boys have been more diligent since they have held their meeting. The dressing is done on the owner's account. The 'buckers' are paid by the barrow 3½d for each. They can break about three in a day. The lead requires to be bruised to a much finer size than the copper ore. The 'cobbers' are paid by the day.

He first went underground himself at 11 years of age in Wheal Gorland at the 45 fathoms level and stayed there for two years. He did not suffer. The first notice he had of his being affected by poor air was feeling one day quite tipsy after drinking a pint of beer. He could before have drunk a pint of spirits without being intoxicated. He has chiefly worked in lead mines and generally on the surface. He is 44 years old and is not aware of any mischief arising from the lead. There are no sores on his feet.

No. 93 Mr. Edward Carthew.
Examined at Balleswidden Mine, April 16th 1841.

He is the agent for the surface work. He has been here for about two years. Previously for five years he had lived on a small farm in Illogan and before that he was for four years and seven months in Colombia under the Colombian Mining Association. Prior to this he has been surface agent at a mine in Camborne parish, between which and his going to Colombia he had stamps of his own.

Have any arrangement different from the system usually followed in the tin mines been introduced here with respect to the employment of the boys and girls? – Some new stamps were set up last October and the number of surface boys and girls has been increasing since. When he went to Colombia he found the method of washing gold ore caused the loss of a considerable quantity which was carried away with the refuse. He was desired to make some improvement in this and set up some 'tyes' in the place of the buddles adjoining the stamps. These were found to be the answer and he has introduced them here. The consequence is that, the work being lighter, the boys at 15s per month can do the work which would have required boys at 25s for the buddles.

What are your hours of work for the boys and girls at surface? – From seven a.m. to six pm in summer and from twelve to one for dinner. On Saturday they leave work at four p.m. in summer and at three in winter.

<u>Is work ever done on the surface after the regular hours of closing?</u> – Scarce ever except at the calcining dressing, which does not employ half a dozen. No work is done on Sunday. The hours of work are seldom shortened by tasks, or in any other way. Working overtime is entirely at their own choice.

<u>Have you observed what is given to the boys and girls for their dinners?</u> – More than half of them have fish and potatoes or stew with a little meat in it. The rest bring pasties or 'fuggans'. A great many have their dinners brought to them warm by their friends from their homes.

<u>Are there any holidays allowed?</u> – Only Christmas Day and Good Friday.

<u>Are the children employed by the tributers or the owners?</u> – They are employed by the dresser who pays them separately. The agreements are made by the children themselves. There is no complaint whatever with respect to the payment of wages either on the part of the children or parents.

<u>Is any check exercised on the tributer as his spaling (fining) the boys under him?</u> – The only spaling practised here is in case of their not coming in time to their work, which is a rare occurrence.

<u>Have you discovered, or have any reason to suspect, dishonesty in many instances?</u> – We have had no reason to complain in this respect.

There would probably be no difficulty in arranging the hours of the children's leaving work so that they might attend evening school.

No. 95. Mr. John Nancarvis, 36 years old.
Examined at the Levant Mine, April 16th 1841.

He is employed as the captain of the dressers and he overlooks the whole of the dressing the copper ores. He has been five years in that situation. Before that he worked underground and had been nearly 20 years under the same adventurers and chiefly in this mine. He has 45 boys and girls under him. The hours of work for the surface workers here are from seven in the morning until 12 then dinner till one and work till five. In the winter, they work as long as they can see....The friends commonly bring their dinners to them, fish and potatoes and stew chiefly. They have holidays in the year and this is an old established custom in the mine. They are not paid for those days. They leave work earlier on Saturdays than on other days and no work is done on Sundays except tending the engine. No boys or girls are employed on that day.

No. 30. Charles Burnet, 36 years old.
Examined Truro, March 10th 1841

He is employed at West Wheal Jewell and has worked here about four years. He over-reached himself in his work after which he brought blood which he has done from time to time since. He has not been capable of working underground since and has an easy place, being employed in looking after the drying of the miners' clothes.

He first went underground at about 12 years of age and worked a year and a half at grass before. He did not feel any ill effects from his working when young. He learnt to read and write a little before going into the mine.

[His complexion is sanguine, pulse haemorrhagic, lungs seriously diseased.]

* * * * * * * * * * * * * * * *

Recollections of the Red River Tin Streams

Captain Benjamin Bennetts [4]

Captain Benjamin Bennetts was manager of a tin stream in the Dolcoath area, on the Red River. It seems that he followed his father as manager, probably in the 1890s and the early years of the 20th century. He was interviewed, in 1952, by a member of the Troon Women's Institute, and his memories were then recorded in their scrapbook. The first account recalls what happened when the Mining Inspector arrived at Camborne Station in order to check safety and employment practices. (This was at a time when many mines continued to employ children illegally, after the Education Acts were implemented by 1880):

[4] Possibly Benjamin Bennetts of Pengegon b. 1856 (1891 Census Camborne 1851/17/4/138) or his nephew b. 1868 (1891 Census Camborne 1851/17/8/140)

'As soon as an Inspector appeared under Brea Arch, word would be passed along, and all the children under age would be sent to hide in the houses, or out into the fields to play.

If there wasn't time to send them out of the way, a bit of dry cloth would be placed on the ground for one or two to sit on, and a kieve turned upside down over them, with a bit of wood about an inch thick pushed under, for air. [5]

Very soon the cab drivers at Camborne station all got to know those inspectors, and the cabbies would arrive on the 'streams' or mines twirling a whip over their heads. [6]

As soon as the inspector was sighted a man would stand on a bank with his right hand behind his back 'every picture tells a story fashion'. This signal would pass up and down ten miles of valley in a few minutes.

The second story illustrates a very strict employment regime, which was commonplace:

'The girls would come to work with clean white aprons and boots shining like glass. If my father saw a girl with dusty boots he would say 'give her notice, she is a bad framer'. The reason being, that instead of using the brush over the frame, away from her, she dragged the brush over towards her - and wasted tin.'

The third recollection conjures up a more pleasant picture of the tin streams working environment:

'The women and children were happy enough. They would start at seven in the mornings and before half past-seven somebody would begin to sing; a hymn or a song.

The singing would be taken up all the ten miles of the valley and it was grand.'

---

[5] See Fig. 11 for kieves at Bissoe Tin Streams.
[6] As a signal that the inspector was onboard.

Fig. 11 Bissoe Tin Stream Works
Courtesy of Cornish Centre Collection

Delabole Slate Dressing Floors and Mill House
Captain John Jenkin

John Jenkin published his detailed account of work at the Delabole Slate Quarry in 1888, where he described himself as a *'Workman on the Quarry'*. He had been born in 1825 in Lanteglos, and had probably been employed as a slate dresser at Delabole from an early age. By 1861 he had moved to take up the same type of work in Tintagel, and seems also to have worked in Carmarthenshire, shortly after. He, subsequently, returned to Delabole and appears to have worked his way up 'through the ranks'. By 1871 he was acting as in some capacity as an agent, although his exact employment status is unclear. By 1881, his younger sons were following in his footsteps, learning their trade as slate splitters at

Delabole.[7] His account certainly indicates an intimate association with the craft. Reproduced here are those parts of his account which describe the work at surface; the dressing floors, and the saw-mills.

Fig. 12 Slate Dressing at Delabole
courtesy of Cornwall Record Office

'*The number of men and boys employed in this quarry may be computed at about four hundred and fifty, and, as a rule, all termed quarrymen. Every class of work has a local name, and the men are distributed over the works as necessity requires....The men that spit the slate [are called] 'splitters'; those that cut or square them, 'dressers'. The boys 'hollobobbers', or 'cullers'; because they pick up the small slate the men pass by. The men who work in the flooring yard are named 'sawers', 'planners', 'loaders', 'cistern makers' etc. There are a number of carpenters, smiths, engine fitters, drivers and a fair sprinkling of foremen. Captain William Lobb has charge of all the hill-men or splitters, sees them in their places, and counts their slates, etc. Phillip Matthews who*

---

[7] 1861 Census Tintagel 1515/8/19/73, 1871 Census St Teath 2221/12/10/43, 1881 Census St Teath 2273/12/137/1

has charge over the boys and looks over their slates to see no inferior ones are passed by for best quality, has also the delivery of powder and safety-fuse to the men. William Knight is foreman of all the flooring department, he counts the number of feet from the quarryman in its rough state, taking orders from the office to the men in the yard, whose duty is also to prepare for shipment. '

'[Splitting requires] still the same old simple plan with only two tools namely, a small mallet with a pair of iron rings locally called a 'beetal', and a steel pointed chisel, about sixteen inches long and about three and a half broad at the bottom end with a round head the size of a shilling. With these two tools a man begins in the morning, and by the time he leaves work he has spit from twenty to thirty dozen of large size slate, a fair days work, although I have known a few men to make or spit as many as a hundred dozen in a day, but it was of extraordinary quality and every preparation that could be done the day before. A man to be a first-class hill-man must not only be a good splitter but must know the true grain of the blocks he has to operate on, and to cut it into proper sizes and thickness previous to it being split into slates. For this purpose a cast-steel set of tools is required, namely a heavy hammer, a gouge for cutting out a groove, and another much heavier one called a cutter, also a very large mallet; with these tools a large block is taken and cut up into proper-sizes; splitting then commences, and by evening a good man has a journey of the best slate ready for the dressing machines. The art of making good slate is in first dividing into the proper thicknesses, say for eight slates. The first split you then have two at four each, take one of them and treat it in the same way you then produce two at two each. The next spit finishes with two complete and proper slates, and so go on through the day....In the evening the men and boys join together and pick up their slates and pitch them in rows by the side of the tram road, they are next loaded into small slate wagons and sent to the machine house. There are four machines of the guillotine type worked by steam, one man superintends each machine. The slate is now cut into various sizes and every size put separate. A large quantity are still cut or dressed by hand in the old way with a horse, fitted with a travel iron and a proper knife, or which is commonly called a zex. Another set of men take the slate down from the dressers and pitch them in rows, and count them in hundreds or 1260 slates, 60 odd being allowed for breakage in carriage. In a row of 100 dozen every 5 dozen is marked by turning one slate about one inch projecting on one side, they are then ready for the market and are easy to count or load. For the above named work the men are all paid at so much per 100 dozen.'

Fig. 13 South Saw House at Delabole
courtesy of Cornwall Record Office

'About twenty men and two horses are employed in the flooring yard and mill house to keep the different machines in operation which are all driven by a powerful steam engine with a main shaft and belt, every machine being connected with smaller ones. There are three circular saws, three hunter saws, a very great novelty to see working, and capable of sawing up the hardest blocks of a foot or more in thickness, drag or water saws cut with sand or water, a rubbing machine for bringing a good surface to head and tombstones, and a very large grinding-stone for sharpening the men's tools, all this work was formerly done by hand labour, at about four times the cost it is done for in the present day. All the above-named work is done by contract at so much per hundred feet for each class of work....The slate dressers are on the same principle, at per hundred dozen, also the filling, landing, emptying wagons, at a fixed price per hundred ton, and for twelve months time.'

Bibliography

Borne, F. W. *The King's Son: A Memoir of Billy Bray* (Bible Christian Book-Room 1872) p. 85

BBP 1842 (Charles Barham) *The Royal Commission for Inquiring into the Employment and Condition of Children and Young Persons in the Mines of Cornwall and Devonshire*

Jenkin, John *Delabole Slate Quarry; A Sketch by a Workman on the Quarry* (Eveleigh 1888) pp. 14-15, 19-20, 22-23

Troon Women's Institute *Troon Scrap-book; Women and Girls on the Mines and Streams* (1952) pp. 4a, 23

Wright, Chris *Billy Bray in His Own Words* (Highland 2004) pp. 53-55, 144-145

Chapter 5

Carn Brea Bal Maidens

During the last quarter of the 19th and first two decades of the 20th centuries, most copper and lead mines in Cornwall had become exhausted, and those tin mines which remained open were severely affected by fluctuations in the world commodity market. Simultaneously, new technological developments resulted in a speeding up the dressing processes, while reducing labour requirements. The combined effect was that vast numbers of mine workers found themselves out of work, in several waves of mass unemployment throughout the area.

All was not gloom and doom, however, as fresh developments in the agricultural and industrial world brought new markets for arsenic (for use in paints and pesticides) and wolfram (as tungsten for hardening steel). Both these minerals had previously been considered worthless, and were either left *in situ* in the mine, or cast aside as waste at surface. Their newly-recognised value meant some mines could exploit these previously unused resources underground, and that others were able to re-dress waste heaps, delaying the time until their final closure.

Another development during this difficult period was a surge in tin stream works. They developed 'on the back' of the deep mining industry, at a time when the technology was not in place to capture, efficiently, the very fine particles of tin now being mined at depth. Tin lost from these mines provided a livelihood for hundreds of women and children in the Red River and Portreath valleys alone. These tin streams also tended to be ephemeral, in that they too were vulnerable to fluctuations in tin prices. However, unlike the deep mines, they required less capital and equipment, and could respond to and exploit market changes more rapidly, offering vital jobs in times of poverty.

County-wide, the over-all picture was of an industry in serious decline and, for the most part, retracting to the central mining district, around Carn Brea. (A few mines remained open elsewhere, most notably on the Tamar, in St Agnes and on the St Just Peninsula). As a result of these widespread closures, the Carn Brea area became the only region where work was still available for women and young people in any significant numbers, whether at surface at the deep mines or at the tin streams. For instance, 820 of the 1,100 bal maidens recorded in the *1891 Census* for Cornwall were living in this area, and by 1901, the numbers were 270 out of 315.

The firsthand accounts in this chapter come from this period of mining history. Most of the recollections come from women who lived and worked at the mines in the Troon area of Camborne, where they were working at some of the largest and most famous mines in Cornwall. Precise dating of their employment is sometimes unclear, but the time span appears to be from about 1870 until 1922. There is also an account of an elderly woman, employed at either the Carn Brea Mines or Carn Camborne, which appeared in Harper's Magazine in 1881. The women whose reminiscences are recorded here, were among the last 'conventional' bal maidens to be employed in Cornwall. They represent the end of an era.

* * * * * * * * * * * * * * * * *

The Troon Bal Maidens

During 1951 and 1952 a scrapbook was prepared, as a county-wide competition entry, by the Troon Women's Institute. It was entitled *'Women and Girls on the Mines and Streams'*. It is not known if it was ever awarded a prize, but it is one of only two such scrapbooks for that year that seem to have survived (the other being for Nancledra, and is held by the Redruth Studies Library). However, to write that the Troon Scrapbook has survived, is not strictly true. Only by the foresight of the librarian at the Camborne School of Mines, who photocopied it in the 1970s, do we still know of its contents. Sadly the original is missing. What follows here is a transcript from that surviving photocopy.

The document appears to have been a scrapbook in the true sense of the word, with handwritten pages of stories and notes, punctuated by photographs, included in a fairly random order. There are quotations from authors such as Leifchild[1] and Hamilton Jenkin[2], interspersed with the

---

[1] Leifchild, J. R. S. *Cornwall, It's Mines and Miners* (Longmans 1855)
[2] Hamilton Jenkin, A. K. *The Cornish Miner* (Allen & Unwin 1948)

memories of women who had worked at the mines or tin streams in their younger days. It seems that these women must have been at least seventy years old at the time of the interviews, and some considerably older.

There are six accounts reproduced here, and they are fascinatingly varied. Mrs. Dalley, was a bal maiden at Dolcoath by the age of ten years old, and was employed there from about 1870. In contrast, Mrs Simms spoke of her time as a spaller at Dolcoath, between 1899 and 1922, almost three decades later. As Dolcoath closed in that year, she must have truly been one of the last bal maidens employed in Cornwall. Mrs. M. J. Collins had worked at Wheal Grenville from the age of 11 years, where her work was serving the buddles. Mrs Gay remembered her sisters working at West Wheal Seaton during the 1880s, and also described her own time at Trevarno Tin Streams (the only one interviewed to have worked at a tin stream). In a slightly different vein, Mrs. Betty Webb described what it was like to be one of the maids at Dolcoath Counthouse. Finally, we have the memories Mrs. Rickard (the daughter of the Dolcoath assayer, Mr. Charles Davis) whose detailed description of the work of her father's highly-skilled assistant, Miss Bickerleg, gives us a rare insight into the world of the sampling room.

The scrapbook included twelve photographs, ten of which were annotated. Unfortunately, the fine detail is lost in the photocopy. Two of the pictures are included in these transcriptions, using good quality images from the Cornwall Studies Collection, and adding the annotations from the scrapbook. Background information which had been added by the interviewers or the scrapbook editor, is retained in parenthesis.

A Dolcoath Bal Maiden 1870
Mrs. Dalley

Mrs. Dalley was born at Carwinnen in 1860. Carwinnen is about a mile from Troon and three from Dolcoath Mine. She died a few years ago – nearly ninety. To me, her early life appeared to have been hard but I never heard her complain even when telling me the following story:

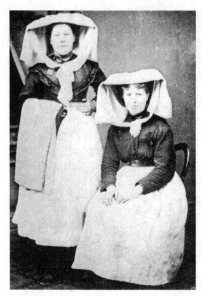

'When I was eight years old I went to Condurrow, nursemaid to Mrs. Williams children. When I was ten I went to Dolcoath Mine to work. I wanted to go to earn some money because, before, I was only getting my keep. I started with 1/- a week.

I used to leave Carwinnen at six o'clock in the mornings. It was alright in the summer, but in the winter mornings I was afraid of the dark. When I got to Troon the children used to come along from Black Rock and Bolenowe. We used to lead hands and sing to keep our spirits up. Sometimes when we got to the bal the water was frozen over. I have cried scores of times with wonders in my fingers and toes'.

Fig. 14 Two Dolcoath Bal Maidens
courtesy of Cornish Centre Collection

[Mrs. Dalley spoke in a rich dialect; the first sentence should be "When I were eight ear old I went Condurra cheelsmaid."][3]

A Dolcoath Bal Maiden 1899
Mrs Simms

'In the years up to 1904 they did not have crushers worked by steam in the mines to crush the big stones of tin ore before it went to the mill or what we call the stamps. They used to employ young women to break up the stones, or, spall them as we called it then. There was a large piece of ground paved for a floor, with a roof to keep them dry.

The stones were brought up from underground and dumped on these spalling floors, and the girls with long-handled hammers broke the stones into small pieces. Then they were taken away to the mill to be crushed or stamped fine so that it could be treated to get out the pure tin. The girls used to wear long white jackets with a 'towser' in front of them, and white bonnets that would come right around their ears, tied under the chin. They also wore heavy boots, heavier than men wear today.

---

[3] Troon Women's Institute Scrapbook p. 9a

I remember going down to Dolcoath Mine many times with my father. He worked in the carpenters shop, and I would spend the day looking around the Bal as we called it then. Many days have I spent watching the female spallers breaking the stones.

In the year 1899 I started to work at Dolcoath but there were not many spallers there then as they had just put in crushers which were worked by steam. Later they worked them by electric. I worked at that mine from 1899 to 1922 when the mine closed down. These were the same class of spallers at the other mines. I remember them at Wheal Grenville, the Basset Mines, and Condurrow.

It used to be a grand sight to see them work, and they were all jolly and bright. They would frighten the people today. I can remember a good many mines working in this district. I can remember when men only got £3 a month and only paid once a month. They were calendar months, on a certain date each month, so that sometimes these were five weeks in a month, but they only got the same pay.

I went to work at Dolcoath in 1899. Then they paid the men and women once a fortnight on the Saturday. Once a fortnight most of the men would get 30/-, and the other fortnight they would only get 28/- as 2/- was kept each month for doctor and club. Women only got £2 per month. Of course the tradesmen; carpenters, masons, smiths etc. got a little more. If a man got £4 a month he would be a clerk or boss or something. In 1920 when the Workers Union was formed they put up the wages. In 1921 I got £4 a week for two or three weeks. Then the mine closed down, and we were out of work. It wasn't long before all the mines around closed down.'[4]

[Contributed by Mrs. Simms. Written down by her husband, and recorded in the scrapbook by LAE.]

A Wheal Grenville Bal Maiden
Mrs. M. J. Collins

'I started work at Wheal Grenville when I was eleven. We girls started at seven every morning and worked until half past five. Whit Mondays and

---

[4] Troon Women's Institute Scrapbook pp. 10-12

Midsummer days we started at 5 to leave off at eleven but then sometimes it was nearly twelve before we could leave work. I can remember hurrying home to wash and change and have dinner in time to walk with the schools.

We worked very hard. Sometimes I must have lifted hundred weights in a day. The buddles used to fill up and had to be cleaned out three times a day. They had to be cleaned out about half past nine, then again before dinner and again in the afternoon. Four men cleaned out the buddles. They wheeled the head to me in a wheel barrow and I had to return it to the buddle again for another washing. That was done three times, then it had to be taken to the packing house. I liked a sharp shovel, the sharper the better. I used to take mine to the men to be sharpened.

Sometimes we had to help the men. We filled the kieves with water from the launder and then carried a kieve of water across to the men, as much as two of us could lift.

I had two brothers and six sisters. My mother used to send hot dinners every day. We always had plenty of good food. We had pigs and fowls and plenty of milk. We had potatoes from the garden. Father always said 'Give them plenty to eat, they can dress up when they get their own living.' I started work for 1s 6d per week. When I was seventeen I had 18s per month. I left and went into service because that was not enough money.'[5]

[Account from Mrs. M. J. Collins – written by Mrs. A. M. Stone]

A Bal Maiden at Trevarno Tin Streams c. 1880
Mrs. A. Gay

'In the year 1875 when I was nine years old I was living at Vyvians Row, Camborne. It was my job to take dinners to my sisters, who both worked on the mine at Wheal West Seaton. One of my sisters was a spaller, and the other a picker. Mary was the spaller who used to break the rocks with a hammer or sledge after it was brought from underground, before going from picking and stamping.

I well remember her wearing a bonnet which was called a 'Bal Maiden's Bonnet'. My sister when she washed and starched it used to make me

---

[5] Troon Women's Institute Scrapbook pp. 16-17

stand very still while she 'styled' it in my head, which means bending it slightly and tying the starched strings so that the bow should not be creased.

She also wore hand-cloths which were made out of white stockings, wrapped round and round the hand and stitched together. The stockings were not worn as long as they are today, so they made a thumb-piece out of a piece of calico. The girls on the mine used to be very careful of their complexions and their hands and on Sundays used to dress like film stars.

My other sister was a 'picker', her job was to pick the good ore from the not so good. The ore was placed on long tables called picking tables and a row of girls would sit on each side and separate it before the ore was sent on to the stamps.

I well remember once a girl going for a drink of water, which was kept in a tin pitcher, when the man who was looking after the girls thought she was going to drink too often, he picked up the pitcher and threw the contents over her, saying' have 'ee had enough now?'

I have in my possession a 'Bal Maiden's Bonnet' made by a lady who used to live in Camborne, who is now dead. She worked at West Wheal Seaton with my sisters.

When I was considered old enough to work I went to Trevarno Tin Streams. [She was living at Plantation, near Troon]. There I used to attend to frames and run errands for the Captain. I remember being sent home once for throwing stones in the flushet. The flushet was like a solid gate which worked up and down, between slides. It was worked by a long screw and handle and was at the end of the slime pit.

I also remember how the girls used to 'swap' or change dinners, one with the other. If one had a 'plum hogan' they would share half of it with someone lucky enough to have had a hot dinner brought. I still remember Annie Tippets potatoe onion and beefee [sic] pasty as she would call it. In the year 1887 I left the streams and went to work at the Tucking Mill Fuse Factory. That was in Jubilee Year, the pay was 4½ per day.'[6]

---

[6] Troon Women's Institute Scrap-book p. 20-22

Fig. 15 Dolcoath Assayer Mr Charles Davies, and Surface Workers
(Mr Dennis and Mr Sims 2nd & 3rd from left, back row)
courtesy of Cornish Centre Collection

At Dolcoath Counthouse
Mrs. B. Webb

'Four women worked at Dolcoath Count House when I was there. Their work was similar to any person in service. Each person had her own job. There was a cook and a girl to help on the kitchen. The others cleaned the rooms of the Managers and the Clerks, and the bathrooms. On Mondays the towels and tablecloths were washed and ironed. Every day we cooked lunch for the Captains and the Clerks.

On 'Sist[7] *days the men had part of their pay that was on the first fortnight every month. Then we cooked a special roast dinner. Full pay came once a month and then a big dinner was cooked for the Managers and Clerks and the underground shift Bosses and the Surface Captains.*

---

[7] Subsist (subsistence): ahead payment of wages in case of need.

However, all the women worked hard. We all looked forward to the Saturday before Christmas when Christmas dinner was eaten. On the Friday we often worked until 10 o'clock. The best tablecloths and glasses and the silver made the tables look very nice. I remember that for one Christmas dinner we cooked a boiled turkey, 3 roast geese, some chicken and roast beef and vegetables. Also we had afterwards a Christmas pudding and all kinds of fruit. There were drinks and smokes. When the men left, the women used to have their dinners. We worked hard but we enjoyed ourselves.'[8]

Taking Dinner to the Mine
(in the Sampling Room)
Mrs. Rickard

In the year 1882 a little ten year old girl could have been seen frequently trudging along the road between Troon and Dolcoath Mine, carrying a basket covered with a white cloth. She was carrying a mid-day meal to her father who worked at the mine, very often it would be a nice, hot savoury pasty.

A child of the same age today would regard such a walk as more or less a punishment but it was a very pleasant change for a little girl who would, very likely, otherwise be helping her mother housekeep for a family in which there were nine children.

Her father was an assayer at the mine which meant she had to go to what was known as the Sampling Room. This was a large room, which had a huge fireplace at one end. All round were shelves and a long table filled the centre. Square pieces of thick white paper, almost like parchment, each about a foot square were arranged on the shelves and the table. These each held a sample of tin ore with the name and working position in the mine of the man who had submitted it, to be smelted to find the value of tin contained.

Each one had to be separately smelted in a container shaped like a flower pot made of earthenware, greyish green in colour, glazed and specially treated to be resistant to the terrific heat needed to separate the tin from the other materials. These containers were known as crucibles.

---

[8] Troon Women's Institute Scrap-book pp. 18-19

The little girl made a friend of her father's assistant, a lady named Miss Bickerleg, who always wore a black dress, well covered with a large white apron and a 'Bal Maidens' bonnet to protect her hair.

Sometimes she would allow the child to stay a little while and watch her at work, carefully brushing every scrap of tin from the crucible onto a very small pair of brass scales, the size of a child's toy. She would say *'We must be very careful about this, my dear, as it means the men's living'*. Instead of using as might have been expected a brush she used a hare's foot explaining that it was so fine no tin would be held in it, to cause any waste. The tin was then placed in an envelope with the weight, value of the sample and the man's name and working position written on it to correspond with that on the paper square.

The mine captains would be walking in and out picking up samples here and there. Miss Bickerleg had the reputation, among the men with whom she worked, *'knowing a much about tin as they did'*.

When she had to leave the sampling room the little girl would walk along to where the girls and were at work on the frames and the buddles, wearing large white aprons and bonnets.

Today she is nearly eighty years of age but still remembers very vividly impressions made when taking dinner to her father as a child. She often remarks on the very low wages paid in those days to a man of her father's knowledge and experience. When he first married he could only earn, as a rule, about 40s per month.

She remembers being given a discarded pair of scales to play with. As soon as these became at all worn a new pair was put in into use. Her father would have to give orders for new crucibles when they were needed. She still has in use one of a set of jugs which were given him, made of the same material and finished as were the crucibles.[9]

[Story told by Mrs. Rickard, aged 80 years. Recorded by Mary Edwards]

* * * * * * * * * * * * * * * * *

---

[9] Troon Women's Institute Scrapbook pp. 13-15

The Old Woman at Carn

This final conversation, recorded here, was between an American writer and journalist, and an elderly woman employed at 'Karn' Copper Mine.[10] In 1881, the journalist William Rideing, was travelling around Cornwall with friends, one of whom appears to have been the artist, B. S. Reinhart. They encountered the woman loading wagons with ore-stuff, ready to be taken to the copper crusher. On returning home, Rideing wrote of this meeting, in a subsequent edition of Harper's Magazine. As yet it has not been possible to identify this woman with any certainty, but a sketch of the group of women, by Reinhart, was published in the article and is included here.

* * * * * * * * * * * * * * * *

'Picking our way through the purplish mud and stones below Karn [sic], we discovered a little old woman labouring over a pile of unmilled copper ore. We had to look twice before we could assume ourselves of her sex: not only was her dress perplexing, but there was an unreality and weirdness in her person. She was very small, almost dwarfish, with bent shoulders and wrinkled hands and face, her skin had the texture of parchment, and was curiously mottled blue, her hair was thin and wiry.

She seemed very old, but her eyes had a shrewd and penetrating quickness, and her movements were utterly without decrepitude. Indeed she applied herself to her work with a willingness of a strong young man, and the work consisted of shovelling the heavy blocks of ore into a small wagon resting on a temporary tramway. Shovelful after shovelful was thrown in with an easy muscular swing, and with much more activity than the average 'navvy' exhibits. Her petticoats ended above the ankle, and were stained with the hue of copper ore; her shapeless legs were muffled up in woollen wraps, and her feet encased in substantial brogans. She was not apparently uncomfortable bodily, but her face had in it a look of uncomplaining suffering, of unalterable gravity, of a habituated sorrow which had extinguished all possibility of a smile. Not understanding a question we put her, she used the words, *"Please Sir?"* – a form of interrogation which we often heard in the neighbourhood of Redruth.

---

[10] Probably Carn Brea Mines or Carn Camborne

Fig. 16 Bal Maidens Spalling and Loading Copper Ore
B S Reinhart, Harper's Magazine 1881

"You seem too old for such hard work" we repeated.

"Deed Sir, I don't know how old I am, but I have been at it forty years. I'm not young any longer that's sure," she answered in a clear voice with scarcely any accent.

"Are you married?"

"No, sir, nobody would ever have me," she continued, without relaxing from her gravity or delaying her work for the moment, *"nobody would have me or go with me, as I was always subject to fits – terrible they are, I still have them once a week sometimes, always with a change in the moon."*

"How do you account for it?"

"Why, before my twenty-fourth year I was in the service of a lady, who threw me down stairs, and that changed my blood; so, when the moon changes, I have the fits. Little can be done for them when the blood's changed."

This superstition was a matter of profound faith for her, but otherwise her manner was remarkably intelligent. She told us that her wages were fourteen pence - twenty-eight cents - a day; and we unnecessarily said that she must be tired of work at such a price, she answered, in a bitter tone:

"No use being tired; when you are tired, there's the workhouse for you."

She had nearly filled the wagon by this time, and two younger women, dressed as she was, but more vigorous looking, came to help her, and after spitting on their hands, which were as large and hard as any man's, they applied themselves with shovels to the heap of ore, falling into a machine like swing of the body as they scooped up the heavy rock. Two men then joined them, and when the wagon was loaded, they propelled it along the track toward the mill, the women sharing the work equally with the men, if indeed, they did not use even greater exertions.'

* * * * * * * * * * * * * * * * *

Bibliography

Troon Women's Institute *Troon Scrap-book; Women and Girls on the Mines and Streams* (1952) (Photocopy and transcript at Camborne School of Mines Library, Penryn Campus).

Rideing, William *In Cornwall with an Umbrella* Harper's New Monthly Magazine CCCLXXVIII November 1881 pp. 807-813, or **Ludlum, Stuart D.** (Ed.) *Exploring Cornwall 100 Years Ago* (Thames and Hudson 1985) pp. 16-19.

Chapter 6

Living a Long Life

Although surface workers at the mines in Cornwall were not exposed to the continual dangers of underground employment, it was not the easiest or the safest environment in which to work. Certainly until the beginning of the 20th century, operations at surface were often designed in a very 'Heath Robinson' fashion. Old equipment and buildings were modified for new purposes, and additional areas were developed in a 'make-do and mend' sort of way (for instance, see the 'lash-up' of tins on a wheelwright constructed wheel in the Frontispiece). As a result, these areas were difficult, or even dangerous, to move around. Health and Safety was not a huge concern; employees were expected to be their own 'safety monitors' and act carefully and sensibly at all times, even if the worker was only eight years old and longing to run around and play. Quite often, expensive machinery was afforded more protection from the weather than those who operated or worked near it. The weather conditions were not kind to the working environment either; mud and surface water prevailing in wet weather, and dust clouds when it was dry. In addition, many of the mines and stream works were in very exposed places (out on bleak moors or cliff tops).

So challenging was the environment, that one suspects it was a 'kill or cure' situation. Susan Robins (as described in this chapter) tells of how desperately tired she was after a day's work when she first went to Wheal Kitty at the age of six. She was tough, and survived. For those with a weaker constitution, the struggle would be on. George Henwood (in an article for the Mining Journal in 1858)[1] implied that bal maidens often did not survive, and many died from consumption. The disease was rife within the mining communities, and so exposures to wet and damp would not help affect a cure, but could only exacerbate the condition. In contrast, Mrs. Bray, writing in the 1830s, expressed the opinion that '*no person born and bred on Dartmoor was ever known to die of pulmonary consumption*' (a place where women and children were working at surface at the mines).[2] In 1903, research by Dr. Pearce seemed to

---

[1] Henwood, George *The Bal Maiden* Mining Journal Vol. 16 p. 36
[2] Mrs. Bray *The Borders of the Tamar and Tavy'* Vol. 1 p. 12

confirm this observation, noting that in some Dartmoor parishes there had been no deaths from consumption in ten years.[3] It seems that in certain circumstances, the bracing nature of the work and exposure to the elements actually enabled surface workers to keep fit and healthy. Despite the premature deaths, there seems to be a significant number of ex-bal maidens who lived into incredible old age.

Reproduced here, are the accounts of two such women. The first is from Susan Robins (nee Wills) of St Agnes, who lived to the age of 101 years. When she was interviewed for the West Briton on both her 100th and 101st birthdays (in 1935 and 1936 respectively) she recalled her early years at surface and the struggles of their life as a mining family. The second is from Mrs. Minnie Andrews of Beacon, who was interviewed for an article in the Cornishman, when she was in her early nineties (in 1967). At the time it was thought that she might be the last surviving bal maiden, but this is by no means certain, as Minnie, herself, refers to another ex-bal maiden whom she believed to still be alive. Subsequently, the article caught the eye of the late Justin Brooke, one of Cornwall's eminent mining historians, and he interviewed Minnie, a few weeks later. His transcript is included here.

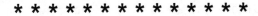

A Wheal Kitty Bal Maiden
Susan Robins (nee Wills) 1835-1936

The two interviews with Susan which survive give us a rare insight into the home and work of mining families during the Cornish equivalent of the Irish Potato Famine of 1847. With the potato and turnip crops failed (the two staple foods), many were driven to despair – and migration. Susan's father (Captain Benjamin Wills) did not take work overseas, but continued to try and earn a living in Trevellas Coombe, St. Agnes. Susan describes how, they had to be up at 4 am to knit socks before leaving for work at the mine at 6 am. This was to earn precious extra pennies to buy food. Her memories of starting work as a bal maiden at the age of six years old, are also unique.

---

[3] Le Messurier, Brian (Ed.) *Crossing's Dartmoor Worker* (1992) p. 131

Cornish Centenarian Who Came from St. Agnes

"I can't tell how it is I've lived to be 100," says Mrs. Susan Robins to a West Briton representative, when he called on her at her moorland home at Minions, near Callington. A delightful little lady, nimble, active, upright, she celebrated her centenary on Monday. *"All I say is I've taken care of myself. I've worked hard all my life. I've gone to bed early, and risen early. I've kept pretty much indoors out of danger. That's the best recipe I can give for old age. No doctor has ever visited me for illness. I've never had a bottle of medicine in my life. I don't believe in medicine. The local doctor called the other day. He was tired, he said. You wouldn't be tired if all your patients were like me, I told him".*

"And would you care to begin again?" she was asked. She smiled.

Fig. 17 Susan Robins (née Wiils) on her 100th Birthday

"No, I don't think I should," she decided at length, *"at least, not under the same conditions. You see, I am one of eleven children. My father was a miner. He only earned 15s a week, and yet he reared a family. He taught us to read and write. I can picture him now, writing with a smutty stick. I went to work when I was six. About twenty of us, boys and girls, 'dressed' tin at works near St. Agnes beacon. I left home every morning at six, walked three miles to work, and trudged home again, at six in the evening. Long hours were they with never a thought of a holiday. Our wages were tuppence ha'penny a day, and if we happened to be a few minutes late or dawdled at work, we were 'docked'* [4] *a quarter! Times were hard in those days. Often there was little food to eat, but we were happy and contented. No, we never needed a doctor. We couldn't afford to!*

My mother had all sorts of pet recipes and knew what herbs to prescribe for a cold or other ailment. Those were the days of crinoline and the poke bonnet. They were my wedding garments when I was married at Stoke Damarel Church, Plymouth, seventy-five years agone."

---

[4] 'Spaled' or fined

"Are you tired of life?"

"*Not likely,*" replied this hale and hearty centenarian, whose intellect is unimpaired. "*I don't want to leave yet. I want to go on working to the end, and when the end comes, I hope it won't be more than a day's illness.*"

She told our representative of how she rises at 7.30 as regularly as the farmer milks his cows. She dresses herself, tidies her room, washes the dishes, helps to prepare the meals, and only wishes she could stand at the wash-tub or scrub the floors as she did not so very long ago. Then, up to bed at nine sharp! Her eyes have become dim, and her hearing is slightly affected otherwise she is healthy, walks as upright as a soldier, eats, drinks and sleeps well, repeats hymns and poems she learnt in her girlhood, and bears little sign of great age.

Unlike most natives of Cornwall, she has no use for superstition, and scorns the power of the ill-wisher and the charmer. She admires the home-loving woman, the woman who sews and knits and does her own housework and puts her children early to bed. "*There is too much 'gadding about' today,*" she said, "*too much dancing and card-playing, too much pleasure. I've never been to the 'pictures', and I've only rode in a motor car once, and yet I've always been happy and found plenty to do in the home.*"

There was great rejoicing in that humble dwelling on the bleak, cold, wild, Cornish moors, on Monday, when Mrs. Robins gathered her five grown-up children, relatives, and friends around her to celebrate her birthday. Her only son, Mr. James Robins, came from Lisbon for the great event. There was a 'whopper' cake with 100 candles. What a time Mrs. Robins had lighting them all, and how delighted she was to be able to cut the cake herself.

Born in St Agnes district, Mrs. Robins is loyal to the county of her birth. She began life on a farm in a mining locality, and she is ending her days in like scenes. *Other places, maybe, have their attractions,*" she says, "*but give me Cornwall every time.*"

A Long Memory; Cornish Centenarian Recalls her Childhood

"The years fly by now – different from the dreary days of the Hungry Forties, when I was a girl." This is what I was told by Mrs. Susan Robins, of Minions, Cornwall, who was 101 years old on Wednesday. Born at St Agnes when King William the Fourth was the reigning monarch, this remarkable old lady has lived through what is probably the most momentous period of English history. One of the eleven children of a Cornish tin miner, whose wages of 15s weekly were insufficient to buy more than bare bread for his large family, Mrs. Robins was sent to work as a 'bal maiden' in a mine when she was six years old, washing and dressing tin at 2½d per day. Out of this fines were deducted for lateness and idleness at work.

"I had to walk three miles to the mine," she told me, *'and it meant starting at six in the morning in all weathers. Before setting out, however, we were not allowed to waste our time so as a whole family we would sit around the kitchen table at four in the morning, knitting the striped stockings which nearly everyone then used to wear. We worked by the light of a tallow candle, and were paid a penny for every ounce of wool we knitted. I had time to go to school for a short time, but I never wrote a line, and my father taught me to write with a bit of burnt stick. We had very little to eat in those days not like the children of today who are never hungry and never have to worry about the next meal. Bread and swedes we lived on chiefly, and sometimes we had pilchards when the farmers went to St Agnes to fetch fish to manure their land. They let us go behind their cart and pick up any fish that were shaken off into the road. Today, I can't touch brown bread – we had so much of it, made with coarse bran that now it makes me sick."*

Mrs. Robins has never had a days illness in her life, except childish complaints which her mother cured with herbs and country remedies. Seventy-six years ago she was married at Stoke Damerel Church to a Devonport dockyard worker, and has vivid recollections of the poke bonnet and crinoline she wore for the occasion. Of her eight children, five are alive. She lives with two of her daughters and her son-in-law, who are all extremely proud of the old lady and careful not to allow her to do too much. This is rather a problem, for Mrs. Robins is as active as many a woman of seventy. She rises in the morning as soon as her son-in-law has brought her a cup of tea. This may be at six o'clock, or even earlier, but ten minutes afterwards Mrs. Robins is dressing. She has never been known to be later than seven. Although her window faces the bleakest part of the Cornish moors, where in winter the wind is bitter, she never washes her face in anything other than cold water, and has never had a hot water bottle. If, by the time she is dressed, her daughters are not up, she calls them. Then she busies herself with household duties. When I saw her she had just finished peeling two gallons of apples, and was looking round for the next job. Before she goes to bed at nine o'clock, she walks around the house and makes sure all the windows and doors are fastened securely.

"Go to bed early, and get up early. Don't worry, and you'll live to be a hundred," she told me. *"people rush about too much these days. Changes are upsetting too. I have never had a holiday in my life, for there is nothing to me like my own bed."*

$$* * * * * * * * * * * * * *$$

Minnie Andrews, the 'Last Bal Maiden'

These surviving interviews with Mrs. Minnie Andrews are also unique as, in part, they have been preserved in the dialect in which she spoke. This gives us a wonderful insight into some of the language of the dressing floors, which is certainly different from the language used by mining engineers and technologists when they described the processes to their scientifically trained audiences. For instance, she describes how she would *'buddly in the strip'*. This was the work carried out to keep a steady supply of tin-stuff flowing from the strips (collecting pits) below the stamps on to the buddles. More formally, this was usually referred to as 'serving the buddles'. The two interviews with Minnie (along with the Troon Scrapbook) have led to the preservation of a unique part of Cornish history; the life of women working on the tin and copper dressing floors, and tin streams at the turn of the 19th and 20th centuries. Although Minnie did not speak very much about the technical aspects of her work, we learn much about working conditions and working relationships.

Minnie was born Minnie Richards, daughter of Richard and Jane, and was living at Carn Entral with her family, according to the 1881[5] and 1891[6] census records. By the time Minnie was nine years old her father was working intermittently, due to ill health. As a result, she had to find employment to help support the family. It seems that she worked at the mines and tin streams over many years being employed at Carn Brea, Carn Camborne, Dolcoath, and West Wheal Francis Mines, as well at

---

[5] 1881 Census Camborne 2336/17/9/88.
[6] 1891 Census Camborne 1851/17/11/142.

Betty Adit, Dick Old's and Rodda's Tin Streams. During this time, she worked at a variety of dressing operations involving both tin and copper ores. Minnie did not marry until 1914, when she was 38 years old. She married widowed tin miner, Richard Andrew. At the time of her marriage she was unable to sign her name; presumably a consequence of her having to work at the mine from an early age. She would probably have been one of the many 'under-aged' children employed illegally at the mines during the 1880s. Although Minnie died within a year of the interviews, in her early nineties, she had remained independent and active almost all her life.

The two interviews reproduced here, both took place in Minnie's home at 38 Fore Street, Beacon, in 1967. The first was published in the Cornishman in April of that year (in which it appears that Minnie's speech patterns have been edited). About six weeks after the newspaper article was published, Mr. Justin Brooke tape-recorded a further conversation with Minnie. His transcription of that second interview is included here, in which he carefully retained Minnie's own dialect. The only editorial changes in this version are the omission of a few phrases where Minnie made an observation, which she then corrected. Mr. Brooke's comments or clarifications are in parenthesis.

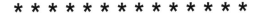

92 year-old was a Balmaiden: Mrs. Minnie Andrews of Beacon

Perhaps the last of the balmaidens, certainly one of the last - Mrs. Minnie Andrews, of 38 Fore Street, Beacon, has just celebrated her 92nd birthday. Her memories of the long closed Wheal Francis and Tincroft and of the tin streams from Betty's Adit down Brea Valley are as clear today as when she walked the tops of the hedges to reach work during the great blizzard of 1891.

Born in a house adjoining Beacon Square, she has lived in the village all her life. Her early years, the years of working and then of family rearing, have all revolved around mining. Even now she has a daily reminder, the castellated stack of Carn Camborne.

As she sat in her chair by the fire in her front room she pointed to the famous landmark across the road. She said, *'I was five years old when I first took father's crowst across to Carn Camborne'*.

A few years later, she was certainly not more than 12, she started work with other local girls at Wheal Francis across from Condurrow towards Peace.

'We walked across the moors to be there for 7 o'clock start in the morning,' she said, *'we had 20 minutes crowst time and half an hour for dinner and we worked through till after five o'clock. My pay? When Wheal Francis closed and I was 18, I got a month just one shilling for each year of my age. I got just 18s a month and I worked harder than some of the men.'*

Mrs. Andrews recalled the names of several Beacon girls, all of whom are now dead, who were inveigled into going underground at Tincroft

Fig. 18 Minnie Andrews, née Richards, 1967 the 'last bal maiden'

when she was working there, and Capt. Arthur Thomas was in charge. *'They could not persuade me to go below,'* she said, *'and I was glad enough when I saw them come back to the surface, sick as shags with fright. The man who took them down came in for a real old rousting from Capt. Arthur, I can tell you'.*

She went to the tin streams, again working alongside the men *'and often harder than they did'.* Betty's Adit were the first streams and a call in at Brea was no rarity. Her aunt lived in the row of houses just down from the inn and 'balmaid' Minnie used to slip in there occasionally with some of the other girls *'for a quick penny glass of porter, but I never liked the stuff'.*

Marriage brought family, three children and an end to mine working for the new Mrs. Andrews. But the connection with mining continued. Her husband was at Tincroft when she first met him. He was in his 70s when he died 17 years ago. One daughter also died and now the other daughter, Mrs. Myrtle Nancarrow slips in daily to help her mother as much as she can. The only son, Mr. Sam Andrew now in retirement from Holmans, lives in Dolcoath Road.

A while back a breakdown in health meant a spell in Barncoose Hospital for Mrs. Andrews, but as soon as she was well enough - some nine weeks - she was back home. Her independence had led her to demand the return. *'Can't stand hospitals,'* she said, describing her plans for walks in the sun this coming spring and summer.

Interview conducted by Mr. Justin Brooke May 1967

'I worked on a copper mine [pointing eastwards]. *I worked at Tincroft and Carn Brea, Dolcoath; I worked West Frances, so that's the main place I worked, West Frances and Tincroft and Dolcoath, they're the main places I've worked.*

I first went to work when I was nine year old. I was turt[7] to the frames and cleaning the holes and getting the water to run, and taking out gravels out from the holes; it did choke up the holes, you know, they things. Oh, I worked awful hours, mister, because I been dying with the cold, my hands, no wonder they go dead, I didn't, they don't go dead, my lor'.

My wages were about fourteen shillings a month, first, starting, and then we went on till we had eighteen. Then we come to a pound...a month, and then we come to twenty-two shilling. That's the highest we had.

Then I used to buddly in the strip [dressing tin on a buddle] *and used to either work with a shovel in the strip, keeping them going, water coming down, washing it all down and filling up the buddle. A buddle would go round with sweeps to it, and then the young men would clean un up and then I should fill un again. I filled twice a day. Johnny Andrew might say something. Johnny Andrews was the boss at Tincroft.*

I had to go to work; I couldn't stay home, my father was sick, he couldn't work half the time. My father worked at Carn Camborne, and I used to carry me lunch up to un all like that every morning. When I wasn't working I used to carry, when I was young (five year old or six year old) I used to go up with crowst .

I helped an old lady called Anna Sincock pick over copper ore at Carn Camborne. They used to pull down the thing and the water would come down in the strip and wash the copper. We was picking out all the bad ones and letting the best ones there.

I worked down Dick Hole's [tin] *streams. And then I worked down to Rodda's streams, down by the adit.* [Betty Adit or Dolcoath Deep Adit]. *That's the only streams I worked. They two. Dick Hole. You wouldn't look your head off from what you was doing, the old fool would have a stick aimed at ee, or something thrown at ee. Oh, he's some demon, he was, an old thing, he was. He'd thraw a stick at ee. My eldest sister used to*

---

[7] Taught

work there. Bessie she was called, and I used to work there, and I didn't care for nobody and never did.

We wore a towser [pronounced to rhyme with mouser, sacking apron]. I used to come home in the evenings and wash my towser. I never had but one, I was too poor to buy the rest, I tell you true; I never bought but one. I had to wash un every so often, and he was white, he was lovely, he was, he wasn't a white stuff, he's like the hessian bags you do see, and you try wash 'em white, come white lovely. And I used to go Monday mornings with a clean towser on, clean hand-cloths; we put hand-cloths on our hands, 'cause we was proud, we didn't want to soil our hands like that. I had a sun-bonnet, I did, yes, I had a sun-bonnet. Could be pinned round here. When I worked West Frances I had that; no, when I worked to Dolcoath, I had that, and one girl used to work down there was, I believe she's living. She used to pin the bonnet in round, that nobody shouldn't see her face, hardly, or just leave her eyes showing. I used to say 'What's the matter with ee, what art doing that for? Then we see who ee are, my dear woman, what's the matter with ee? She used, she didn't like it, you know, she used to be as vexed as fire.

I'm gone ninety-three, I was ninety-three last birthday, but they some do say, you're ninety-two, Miss Andra'.

Oh, a lot of people were working at Tincroft with me, twelve or thirteen, might be more, of women; let's see, there's Margaret Moore, Nellie Instone, that's two, and er, me, that was three, and Liza 'Sick'[8] is four. I can't remember them, but I knew there were a lot; but then when I went to work. I used to go in the dinner-house and...used to get their food ready and the hot [water] and things; used to put their pasties and things in the oven and warm them again and they come in twelve o'clock and get the tea, get their tea ready, and then I used to tell them when it was turn for them to bring their tea. Now I used to say 'You must bring your tea, whose turn is it? You ought [to] know, I ain't got no tea here'. So they bring their tea, like that, and they'd have a good cup of tea and then we used to go on like that.

We worked...from seven to five, that's right, but then we didn't work, sometimes...when we leave off early we used to be all right then, we used to have the hour some day. Johnny Andry [Andrews] he was my boss. He's some wise man, over West Frances, no, Tincroft, that was Tincroft. I worked Tincroft, used to work. You go, we go the places where we gather most money, see? He was a class leader up Pool Chapel; he

---

[8] Eslick or Visick?

was a nice man, Charley Andrews was a nice man. We shan't see they days no more.'

When Minnie died some ten months later, her passing was recorded in the following article in the West Britain:

Started Life as a Balmaiden

In the death at Barncoose Hospital, Redruth, of Mrs. Minnie Andrews, aged 91, of 38 Fore Street, of the village of Beacon, Camborne, loses one of its most notable 'characters'. Like other girls of the village at the time, she started her working life at the age of 12 as a balmaid at Wheal Francis Mine, Peace.

The working day began at 7 am and ended at 6 pm, and the girls were paid 18 shillings a month. Once a week they would call at the Brea Inn for a penny glass of porter. Mrs. Andrews also worked at Tincroft, Betty Adit and Brea Tin Streams, beside the male miners, and often toiling harder than they did.

The funeral took place last week at Troon Cemetery, Mr. Henry Sibthorpe conducting the service. [She was survived by a son and daughter, and six grandchildren. There follows a list of mourners and pall-bearers.].

Bibliography

Brooke, Justin. Transcript of Interview with Mrs. Minnie Andrews (1967)

The Cornishman 6th April 1967

West Briton 31st October 1935

West Briton 29th October 1936 p. 6

West Briton 3rd March 1968 p. 22

Chapter 7

The Glass Mine Women

In Cornwall, wartime sometimes meant that women and girls were recruited to take over vacant posts at the mines and clay works, where men had volunteered for active service. (Generally, miners were not called up, as they were in a reserved occupation, but some left voluntarily). In addition, new jobs were created when existing mines were expanded or redundant mines re-opened, to meet the increased demand for metals and minerals. This was the case at Tresayes Orthoclase Mine, Roche, during the First World War. Thought to be exhausted of good quality potash feldspar (orthoclase) by about 1880, it was reopened in hope when there was a growing need for its use in high quality glass. (Previously, the UK requirements were met by imports from Norway, but with the North Sea blockaded, this was no longer an option). 'Polpuff Glass Mine' (as it was known locally) was certainly in production by 1917 and, probably, as early as 1914. Women were drafted in from the locality for the surface dressing, and about 50 were employed, at the peak of production. The workers at Polpuff believed that the orthoclase was needed for the toughened glass in submarine periscopes. In reality, there was probably a whole range of important uses, including glass for medical instruments (such as thermometers and laboratory equipment). It seems that some of the orthoclase was also prepared for the coal-washing process, and shipped to South Wales. The women at Polpuff continued at their work after hostilities had ceased, until such time the international market had recovered. They were subsequently laid off in 1921.

During 1980, John Tonkin spoke to those still living in the area, about their war work. These women who, by then, were mostly in their eighties, were usually interviewed in their homes. Their memories appear to have been exceptionally good, with most of the information cross-authenticating, (although there was some uncertainty, understandably, around identifying individuals in a surviving group photo). Notes were taken during the interviews, and transcribed into a ledger. It is this ledger record which is reproduced here.

Fig. 19 At the dressing tables, Polpuff
courtesy of China Clay Review

There are six accounts recorded; five from women who worked at the dressing tables and the sixth from the tally-checker (who recorded the number of boxes filled by each individual dresser). John Tonkin's own comments and observations are retained in parenthesis. At the time of these interviews, some of the women were anxious about their identity being made public[1] and undertakings were made about not doing so, in their lifetime. None are alive today, and after careful discussion, it has been decided to name them here (usually by their maiden name, under which they would have been employed). This decision has not been taken lightly, but out of a concern that these women should be recognised for the contribution they made to the war effort all those years ago. We hope that today they would have been able to feel openly proud of their work, and would happily receive the acknowledgement they deserved.

Three photographs have survived from this time. One image shows the women posed at their dressing tables, hammers in hand. Another is a group photograph of 48 female employees, thought to be taken in 1918, and almost certainly at the beginning of the working day. The third image, showing two men and eight women, was possibly taken at a later date than the second photograph (as those who appear in both are dressed differently, and look a little older). Whilst most of the women seem to be in their late teens or early twenties, there were a few of more senior age, and about a dozen who were, perhaps, school leavers (at 14 or 15 years old).

* * * * * * * * * * * * * * * * * *

Interview 208: Hilda Lander

---

[1] This is possibly because they were aware of the stigma that had become attached to female mine workers in Cornwall, by the end of the 19th century

Born in 1897, Hilda worked at Polpuff Glass Mine, Roche for a short time before marriage. During the winter of 1920-1 she remembers ore frozen together and on to the picking table. The ore was trammed down and tipped onto a long picking table. They then picked out the quartz, and broke the mixed material with hammers. They were on task work and each had a set number of boxes to fill per day, and each person had her own numbered box. A man took the full boxes and washed the feldspar in a stream. It was then put out to drain and dry on the bank. The "deads" were thrown in a heap behind the women.

She found work in a knitting factory in Newquay, when the mine closed. She later married a clay worker.

Interview 209: Gertrude (Gussie) Retallick

[Miss Gussie Retallick who worked at the Glass Mine as a tally checker was the daughter of Capt. Fred Retallick. She was visited to obtain as many names of the girls in the photograph of the Polpuff bal-maidens as she could remember (see below). Gussie's memory was good.]

No. in Photo	Name and Details	No. in Photo	Name and Details
1	Mona Rice	22	Miss Hooper
2	Miss Hoare?	23	Miss Yelland (of Tresayse)
3	Hilda Richards	24	Mertle Truscott (of Enniscaven)?
6	? Cutler?	25	Helen Whale
8	? Cutler?	31	? Kellow?
9	Olive Marshall	32	Pearle Yelland
12	Miss Higman (of Luxulyan)	33	Rosie Higman
14	Annie Yelland (of Carbis)	35	Teresa Higman
15	May Currah	36	Hilda Lander
17	? Wilson (of Molinis then Saveth)	37	Blanche Rundle
18	Susie Hooper	41	Elsie Yelland (from Tresayse)
19	Gladis Rowe	44	Mable Varcoe (of Lanivet)
20	Edith Harris?	46	Gurtie Ball (sister of Albert)
21	Gussie Retallick		

The ore was trammed out from the quarry [about which Gertrude knows nothing]. It was dumped on a sloping ramp above the picking bench. It would be drawn down by the women as needed. They had to pick out the yellowish-buff feldspar and place it in a box. There were about 40 on task work, standing in a line. The "deads" were thrown behind the maidens to be taken away at intervals.

Interview 215: Mary Hazel (Hazel) Varcoe

[Born c. 1900. I had interviewed Mr. G in the company of his wife in October 1976, but didn't realize that Mrs. G. had been a bal maiden at the Glass Mine. She didn't quite live up to her promise of being able to name everyone in the photo (see below), of which she has a copy; a couple (of the few) that she couldn't name she remembers the girls, but just can't recall a name.]

No. in Photo	Name and Details	No. in Photo	Name and Details
1	Mona Rice	25	Helen Whale
2	Grace Hoare	26	Ruth Burden
3	Hilda Richards	27	Mary Hazel Varcoe (18 yrs old)
4	Annie Andrew	28	Lily Grig
5	Mrs. Rescorla	29	Mrs May Chapman
6	Nellie? Evacuee from London	32	Pearle Yelland
8	Evacuee from London	33	? Higman
9	Olive Marshall	34	Flossy Andrew, older sister of Annie
10	Flossy Runnals	35	? Higman
12	Mary Higman, the boss	36	Hilda Lander
13	Lydia Dalley	37	Blanche Rundle
14	Annie Yelland	38	Elsie Thomas
15	May Currah	39	Netta Tabb
16	Nellie Hooper	40	Maude Snell
17	A girl called Roberts not Wilson	41	Elsie Yelland
18	Susan Hooper	42	Ivy Simmonds
19	Gladis Rowe	43	Louise Liddicoat (from Nampean)
20	Edith Harris	44	Mable Varcoe
21	Gussie Retallick	45	Beatrice Ball
22	Lilian Hooper	46	Gurtie Ball (sister of Albert)
23	Florence Yelland	47	Eva Gench
24	Myrtle Truscott	48	Beatrice Osborne

Fig. 20 Women orthoclase dressers. Polpuff
courtesy of John Tonkin

[After sixty years, to name so many is a remarkable score for an eighty-year old. This also set me thinking that these maidens worked under conditions that any trade-unionist would not only object to, but would rail against because such conditions would injure health (i.e. either dirty or wet and open to the elements etc.) yet at least one in six is still alive, in their eighties, or close thereto, and the ones that I have seen are very active and young looking. Mrs. G. was out in her courtyard cleaning a bag of potatoes when I arrived.]

The girls "*picked out the quartz from the feldspar*" which they put the ore into wooden buckets with an iron rim, which would contain about 56 lbs. From there it was tipped into the stream for washing prior to shipment. In the winter the ore would stick to the galvanized iron on the bed of the chutes with the frost. Most went to Carbis, for shipment, being carted there, however some was occasionally taken away to an unknown destination [Trelowth?] in wagons pulled by a traction engine driven by Clarence Rosevear. This came from "*Treviscoe Way*".

Hazel's mother was American. Her father returned from America and worked in the family mica-clay dry just up the road 50 yards from where she has lived for the past 50 odd years. They lived very close to the dry. She used to walk to work: out over Tregoss Moor from Enniscaven to the foot of Pitmingle Hill; up through Clears to Roche Church; up the road to Tresayes Chapel; in across to Polpuff and on to the Glass Mine. A long exposed hike in all winds and weathers, "*and never late once*".

Fig. 21 Orthoclase dressers, Polpuff
courtesy of China Clay Country Park Mining & Heritage Centre

Interview 217: Annie Andrew

She lived in Currian Road, and used to walk with five others across fields for work, leaving at 6 am for a 7 am start. She was paid piece work, and sometimes finished by 2 pm.

Interview 218: Pearle Yelland

Born in 1901, she lived at Whitemoor. When she first went to work, there were only a few women working, and left before the mine closed, in about 1918. Eventually more than fifty worked there.

Capt. Retallick was the surface captain and Charles Rosevear the assistant. There were two 'treatment captains', one at the top end of the floors, one at lower end, to make sure no-one disappeared. The ore boxes held 50 lbs. When full they were booked to each girl and then the contents tipped into the leat. The ore was then taken out onto the concrete wharf. It was taken in horse-drawn wagons to be shipped from Carbis. The waste would be tipped through a screen by a boy. The oversized waste would then be repicked and broken. As it would be wet from washing, and yielded less, it was not a favourite occupation. So the women took it in turns. In the summer two or three more skilled girls would work on the wharf, cutting cubes (about 1½-2") which were sent for the coal washing process in South Wales. This took longer - only few boxes were completed per day.

Interview 226: Beatrice Jenkin

Born in 1896, Beatrice was a piano teacher but was called up to work at the mine as essential war work. She disliked it. She was issued with clogs to start with, but the surface was too uneven, so she resorted to wearing her own shoes. She soon wore out jumpers and jackets. The ore boxes were about 18" x 12" x 6".

Bibliography

Mayers, Lynne *Bal Maidens* (Blaize Bailey Books 2008) pp. 126-29.

Tonkin, John Personal correspondence 2003 and 2008.

Chapter 8

At the Geevor Washing Floors

By the end of the First World War, nearly all of the traditional manual dressing tasks on the tin floors, recognisable over the centuries, had been replaced by various mechanical processes. However, one particular task still remained un-mechanised, and that was the sorting out of debris and waste rock as material was brought to surface. This material was now moved around at surface by a series of conveyor belts and wagons, similar to the picking screens of the Northern Coalfields. Whereas girls and women were used for this task in some Lancashire, Yorkshire and Staffordshire coal mines it seems that, in Cornwall, it was the task for the youngest male recruits. Richard Lawry was employed in this way at Geevor, in early 1939, fairly soon after leaving school. With the onset of war, however, his role 'at surface' was soon to change. He was to find himself supervising others at the same picking belt on which he had worked. Latterly he worked at the ball mill, and then on the tin floors (working at the buddles and weighing tin).

Surveys had been made of many of the mines in Devon and Cornwall, at the outset of the Second World War, to investigate whether it would economic to re-open them (to provide much-needed metal ores). It was decided, however, only to invest in those mines which were still in operation. With attempts to increase production, and with some workers volunteering for War Service, women were sometimes called in to fill vacancies at surface. There are certainly records of women being employed at Great Rock Iron Mine in Hennock in Devon, as well as at Geevor Tin Mine in Cornwall. It was these women that Richard Lawry was to be asked to supervise.

Some of the memories of those women who worked at the picking belt at Geevor, have been preserved by the Geevor Oral History Project. A photo of four of the six or seven who worked there, has also survived. One of these women, the late Phyllis Lockett (née Taylor), wrote about working on the picking belt for the author, in 2003. Sadly, she did not live to see her story in print, as she died just a few months before it was published for the first time, in *Balmaidens* [1], in 2004. It is this same story that is reproduced here. In addition, Richard Lawry has recorded his own memories of the washing floors around that time (including when these women first arrived at the picking belt) in his fascinating book, '*Scrapbook of Memories of a Geevor Man - My Early Life*'. His account is also transcribed (slightly edited with his permission), with some additional information he has shared on working hours and pay.

For this war work at Geevor, the hours were changed so that there were two shifts of twelve hours, instead of the normal three shifts of eight, thus reducing the number of employees needed. Although the work was under cover, many aspects of the working environment echoed the conditions of an earlier age. Workers still had to endure almost unbearable noise levels, and even developed their own sign language. They still worked in a very dusty, cold and dirty environment. There were various dangers and challenges; flying shards which flew into the eye, cuts and bruises to the hands, and unsavoury items arriving on the belt from underground, not to mention the occasional 'unofficial' climb on to belts to remove blockages. This work was certainly not an 'easy option'.

* * * * * * * * * * * * * * * * * *

The Recollections of Richard Lawry
Geevor Tin Mine 1939 -1950

'My job was on a slow moving conveyor belt, sorting out 'Deads', black and white spotted granite stones, from the other ore which was on the belt. We placed the 'Deads' down a chute which led to a fast moving conveyor belt which ferried them to an outside dump.

Now the other ore containing tin, copper, glass, spar and gold-coloured mondach headed to another conveyor belt which dumped them into a fast powerful crusher. When they emerged on another belt, they were gravel and dust. This belt dumped them into a large bin which contained three little belts below and into the Ball Mill. There were about 8 or 10 of us 'Boys' on the picking belt. We were under the supervision of an ex-underground miner who had 'Tithus', a miner's lung complaint. He was allowed to finish his remaining years on the surface. Once tin dust gets on your lungs, there is no cure, and there is many a young miner of about 30 or 40 buried in the cemeteries.

---

[1] *Balmaidens* by Lynne Mayers (Hypatia 2004) is now out of print. A second edition *Bal Maidens* was published by Blaize Bailey Books in 2008.

Long hours of staring at the picking belt proved very boring and tiresome. We would walk outside to try to get the blood circulating through our legs again. Oftentimes one felt dizzy. I remember fainting one day – I just dropped to the floor, but went outside for a few moments, then all was O.K. again. The noise of the washer was unbearable. On the picking belt would be items the underground miners lost or threw away. A miner's lamp, knife, tin of 'baccy, iron drills, and smelly carbine, some length of fuses, and detonator caps.

The lengths of fuses and detonator caps we hung up to dry. During the cold winter months we kept an empty 50 gallon oil drum with holes punched in the sides, in which we kept a coke fire burning. There was a bountiful supply of coke and coal which worked the mines steam engines. It was nothing unusual for some guy to put a cap into the fire and blow a hole in the drum. Sticks and timber were plentiful on the belt and we had to pull off large pieces of wood covered with rust coloured slime. We dried them also, for our fire.

Fig. 22 Boys from the picking belt, Geevor 1940
Back row L to R Cyril James, George Maddern, Richard N Lawry,
Norman Polglaze, Herbert Harris, Bobby Thomas (Overseer)
Front Row L to R Penrose Trembath, Alec Osborne
courtesy of Richard N Lawry

I was quick to learn the switches and we boys proved our worth on more than one occasion. Whenever we smelled rubber burning, we knew a motor would burn out if we didn't act fast. We would run for the switches and turn off the danger, and shout an alarm. Within minutes we had corrected the trouble, perhaps a rock had jammed in a pulley, and we were back at full speed again. We were always on the alert for the company's welfare, as our jobs depended on it.

Our mine was booming with a war on and it would soon be going 24 hours a day. By Wednesday or Thursday, often our bins were so full that the gravel and powder was coming up the chute towards the conveyor. Many times in the afternoons, a couple of us…would be ordered up there with a Banjo [2] each. We would spend hours shovelling the ore…to keep the belt clear and running. When we could handle no more, we would signal Johnny Mathews, and give him the 'danger' signal.

As I happened to go to the bins, early one morning, to start the conveyor belt for the beginning of a days work, I looked down and could see the mill's little belt running, but the gravel had backed up. I had no shovel, but knowing it would be perhaps 30 minutes before my plant could begin laying a load up there, I just jumped down unconsciously, not heeding any danger, like most 15 or 16 year olds. I scraped my boots up and down along the bottom until quite a lot of it would give way and come with a rush. Somehow I got pinned under and I could feel my feet go under like quicksand. It was then that I sensed my danger. I had probably started the belt above and that could bring up and dump more on top of me as the other belts down the plant were started. Perhaps I prayed, I don't know, but another boy showed up and without too much panic, gave the alarm, stopped the belt, and rushed down the mill and warned the mill man who stopped the little belt below me. I was extremely thankful when a rope was thrown to me and somehow with help I got out. It was so hush-hush, I don't know if I even thanked the boy.

One day our boss Bob Kessil said that we would be needed a few evenings for just a week or two, a couple of hours each evening to brush and scrape the inside of the boilers and we were to bring some old raggy clothes. It would be worth a few extra shillings in the pay packet. Well, we showed up that first night and saw those big black boilers with the little doors, we could have cried. The old men couldn't have cared less, so inside we had to go. We had to scrape and pass out the soot, eating, spitting, and choking all the time we did it. There were three or four boilers and one boy in each. We took turns, but it was still so sickening. We stuck it out and after a few days we refused to work any more. We were all fired. A few of us were re-employed while others ended up in the coal pits as 'Bevin Boys', and then in the army when 18.

---

[2] Small shovel with banjo shaped handle.

Geevor, like many other businesses, had to seek a way as to shorten manpower because the young men were being called away to the war effort. Geevor did this by placing surface three shift jobs to two shifts, thus disposing of a crew. Two crews had to work twelve hour shifts from 7.00 am to 7.00 pm. This worked on alternate weeks. One day, aged 16, I was asked to show the girls how to tell the difference between granite stone from the others, and what to do with those stones. Then take charge of the operating of the entire plant. I felt very proud just to think, my boss, old Mr. Collins, had liked me enough to trust me in control. Of course it meant doing all the starting and stopping of motors, I loved doing that anyway. Then I would have to watch the bins closely and shovel when needed, also walk around the plant and turn on necessary taps and water valves, clean out launders when overflowing, grease and oil etc. Some of my girls staff were: the boss' daughter Cora Collins, her cousin Bella Prowse, Jean Polglaze, Josephine Mathews, Sylvia Angove, and Phylis Mathews down lower Boscaswell. However, I had my hands full. But I loved it, it was the best job I ever had in the eleven years I had at Geevor.

It was customary for old man Collins to make his rounds every morning around 9 00 am. He would pause on that gang plank, walk towards the bins, and lean over the rail to watch the girls on the picking belt. He always had a smile should he meet me or anyone else.

When the photo was taken [1940] we were paid 2s 9d per day. At six days a week this was 17s 4d. But we left work at 12 noon on Saturdays. The photo was taken in our lunch break from 12.00 to 12.50 pm. We worked 44 hours a week.

One day Mr. Collins beckoned me over and we walked up to the bins away from the noise of the machinery. 'Young man, I have another job for you', he said. 'I would like you to work down below in the ball mill, three shifts. Of course, it pays more money and will advance your experience.'

Mr. Walter Harry of Tregeseal, Mr. Arthur Reynolds and Mr. William Palk of Boscaswell worked the three shifts at the Ball Mill. These men were responsible for the operation of the machinery and keeping a constant watch on the heavy feed which went through launders, humbers, and the revolving mill itself. The mill acted like a crusher. It contained 1,600 steel balls, each weighing 7lbs, and the gravel and water which went through from the previous bins, came out like sand and water. It soon became obvious that further help was needed to keep a steady flow of 'feed' going through the 'gratings' or 'filters' which sometimes would overflow because of small pieces of wood or rag. So it was that I was assigned to Arthur Reynolds.

When on night shift, Bill Palk and Douglas Webber, his day boy, would relieve us at 7 00 am. Instead of racing home, I would walk alongside Arthur. We both lived at Trewellard, Arthur at lower and I up the hill. He could only walk a few yards and then would have to stop to get his breath. When Arthur died I was given his job. I was seventeen years of age. I knew the controls both of starting and stopping, and was capable of responsibility. I felt proud to think that old Mr. Collins and Eddy, his son, trusted me.

When the war was over, I approached Mr. Collins one day and pleaded that he give me a day-shift job. Soon I had my request and was given a job down on the tin floors 8.00 to 5.00. The ore which was blasted, trammed and hauled to the surface, had been crushed, washed, crushed again, then washed and crushed in the mill and now appeared on the tables as shining mud, then into the buddles. Many strong and tough young men were employed on the tin floors. They were strong as horses.

Some men were in charge of 'Kieves', a large wooden barrel containing heavy tin. They had to skim off the top of the 'dirt' which was rebuddled: underneath the 'skim' was pure shiny tin. Carts with two shafts in both front and rear were filled and two men, one on front and one in the rear, would then wash their boots, and carry the cart of tin into the tin house. Once a week when the tin house contained about 30 to 40 tons, a crew of maybe three men were given a day's task to bag and weight it, loading it on to trucks for its journey up north to the factories. Each bag of tin weighed at least a hundredweight, 20 of these and you had handled a ton. Just 30 tons and you have handled 600 bags of heavy tin on the scales and off again. We would begin work on a Monday's task at 7 00 am and finish it at 12 o'clock. Tired and with a two mile hike home. Then too, we had to empty buddles, some with hand barrows and others with wheelbarrows. The wheelbarrows took away the wet slime which slopped down from the heavy tin. Often the tin had to be rebuddled to get out the impurities before it was ready to go into the kieves.

We had a nice dinner house with a fire stone and oven. We had a boy who fetched pails of water for boiling in the large old iron kettle. This boy was also responsible for preventing our 'Pasties' from burning and keeping kettles always boiling for our crews, some would eat at 11 am, others at 12 noon.'

After eleven years working on the washing floors at Geevor, Mr. Lawry left to emigrate to the United States.

* * * * * * * * * * * * * * * * *

The Recollections of Phyllis Lockett (née Taylor)
Geevor Tin Mine, Second World War

'During the Second World War seven of us worked on the picking belt at Geevor Tin Mine, while the men were away. We were all single, except for one who was a widow. Our job was to remove as much of the waste from the tin-bearing ore as possible, before it went to the crushers. We all lived in the village of Geevor. When we started we had no real training; we were just shown what to do by the supervisor.

The hooter sounded at Geevor at 8 o'clock to start work; at 12 o'clock for dinner time, at 1 o'clock to be back at work, and at 5 o'clock to finish for the day. It also sounded at the New Year and any other special occasion. Our normal working day, then, was eight hours, but we had to work late if the plant broke down. We worked a full day Monday to Friday, and then Saturday mornings as well.

Fig. 23 Women at the picking belt, Geevor World War 2
courtesy of Geevor Tin Mine

The seven of us who worked on the picking belt all changed places every hour so that we all took it in turns at the different jobs, including lifting off the large granite stones. Some were very big and could not go down the chute, so they were thrown on the floor to be broken up by the foreman. If a stone got jammed in the washer chute we had to run around shutting down the plant, and then start it all up again when it was clear. The ore-stuff had first come through the washer, so we always had our fingers in water. The other smaller pieces of granite which we picked out were put on another conveyor belt, to be disposed of. This ore was carried to another house where it was delivered down a chute into waiting trucks. This was then on to the crushers.

Sometimes we had to work until 11 pm if there had been a breakdown, so that all the tin was gone from the main bunkers for the night-shift men to have room in their bin. We had plenty of other jobs to go to while the fitter was mending the machinery. One was to clean the tin sacks. This was done on the tin floors, and we used to beat the bags on an iron stand and then pick off the pieces of string. Another job was to get in the bunker and clear out all the tin that had been left in the corners and shovel it through the square holes out to the shaking tables.

The washer and crusher were very noisy, and we couldn't hear ourselves speak. We used to lip read and made up our own sign language. The working conditions were also very dirty. However, we worked undercover, in sheds, so that we were able to work despite weather conditions. Sometimes small pieces of spar would fly up into our eyes, and we would have to go to the first aid post to have it taken out.

There was a canteen at Weatherhead, and we used to have pasties from there, which we ordered early, if we didn't go home for lunch. Sometimes we brought our own lunch. We had our own little tearoom and took it in turns making tea. We took our tea breaks two at a time. We wore our own clothes and shoes to work, and some of us brought clogs, as they lasted longer. We were paid weekly.

Although working on the picking belt was hard work, we all got on well and we all enjoyed ourselves'.

* * * * * * * * * * * * * * * * *

Bibliography

Geevor Oral History Project *Women and Mining CD* (2004)

Lawry, Richard Nicholas *Scrapbook of Memories of a Pendeen Man: Part 1 My Early Life* pp. 21-24, 27 + personal correspondence RNL/LM July 2009

Lockett, Phyllis *At the Picking Belt* (personal correspondence PL/LM 2004)

Glossary

Barrowing: a hand barrow was usually used by the women and girls (one barrow containing 1.5 cwt ore dry weight). Wheel barrows were used by the older boys and men. (Fig. 6 & 11)

Blowing Air: operating ventilating machines below ground (usually by boys).

Buddling (Buddly): a sedimentation technique for separating ore from waste. (Figs. 8 & 9)

Carrying: see *barrowing*.

Cobbing (Cobbie): breaking medium grade copper or lead ore into small pieces with hammers, to separate waste. (Fig. 6)

Croust: mid or late morning break for food.

Dry: shed where miners can change, and dry underground clothes.

Framing: see *recking*

Griddling (Riddling): using a sieve to grade ore or separate waste. (Fig. 6)

Hobban (Hoggan): coarse savoury barley bread. Fuggan is a sweet version with raisins.

Kibble: large iron or steel bucket for lifting ore up from the mine.

Kieve (Keeve): vat or large barrel for washing ore. (Frontispiece & Figs. 7 & 11)

Killas: metamorphosed sedimentary rock in which ores may be found.

Knacked: broken or used up (such as a worked-out mine).

Jigging (Gigging): sieving fine copper or tin-stuff under water in large boxes. (Fig. 6)

Mundic Water: refuse water from dressing operations, containing impurities, often arsenical products.

Picking: separating pure ore and waste from ore bearing material, leaving mixed grade ready for further dressing. (Fig. 6)

Recking (Racking): the finest sedimentation technique for separating tin ore from waste using ragging (racking) frame. (Fig. 7)

Rolling: tramming ore wagons, above or below ground.

Serving the Buddles: ensuring flow of fine tin-stuff or copper tailings from the strips to the buddles.

Slimes: the finest portions of tin-stuff which are to be washed on the frames.

Spalling: breaking larger rock pieces by hammer ready for the stamps (tin) or for the crushers or cobbing (copper and lead). (Fig. 7 & 15)

Stuff: term for impure ore, usually used for tin, rather than copper.

Tea: mugwort or other herbs, used as a tea substitute.

Towser: the bal maidens' apron; usually without a bib, but of good length and width to give coverage. Made from flour bag material, or hessian. (Fig. 14)

Tye: structure for dressing tin, similar to a strip.

Washing Up: washing of ore, usually in conjunction with picking.

Work at Grass: work carried out at surface.

Work for Self: where wages were kept by a child (usually overtime), rather than being given to the parents

Index

Bold numbers refer to Illustrations

Francis, Fanny 39
Friendship, Wheal (Devon) 52
Fuse factory 73

Gay, Mrs 72-72
Geevor Tin Mine 99-106
Gench, Eva 96
Grig, Lily 96
Gorland, Wheal 39, 57
Grenville, Wheal 71, 72
Gwennap 30-32, 36-40, 41-46, 52-54,
  57, 59

Harris, Edith 96
Harris, Herbert **101**
Harris, John 1, 6-11
Harris, William 31
Harry, Walter 103
Hewas, Wheal 14
Hicks, John 55
Higman, Mary 96
Higman, Rosie 96
Higman, Teressa 96
Hitchens, Fortescue 2
Hoare, Grace 96
Hocking, Elizabeth 47
Hooper, Lilian 96
Hooper, Nellie 96
Hooper, Susan 96
Hosken, Captain 53

Instone, Nellie 90

James, Cyril **101**
Jeffery, Richard 45
Jenkin, Beatrice 98
Jenkin, Captain John 61-65
Jewell, Jane 41
Jewell, West Wheal 59
Jigging 6, 10, 32, **33**, 37, 44, 47, 48
Johns, Mary 36

Kenidjack Tin Streams *frontispiece*
Kessil, Bob 103
Kitty, Wheal 40, 81-82
Knight, William 63
Knuckey, Thomas 32

Lander, Hilda 95, 96
Lanner 31, 32
Larkeek, Elizabeth 36
Lawry, Richard 100-104, **101**
Lead dressing 57
Levant Mine 58
Liddicoat, Louise 96
Lockett, Phyllis 105-106, **105**

Lobb, Captain William 62
Luke, John 15

Maddern, George **101**
Manual, Charles 41
Marshall, Olive 96
Martin, John Henry 30
Martin, Thomas Knuckey 32
Mathews, Johnny 102
Mathews, Josephine 103
Mathews, Phylis 103
Matthews, Phillip 62
Mexico 45
Mine Inspector 59-60
Minions 82, 85
Moore, Margaret 90
Morcom, Elisha 45
Morom, Christina 41

Nancarvis, John 58
Nancledra 68

Olds, Dick 90
Orthoclase dressing 93-96
Osborne, Alec **101**
Osborne. Beatrice 96

Palk, William 103
Parish Overseers 14
Pascoe, Christina 44
Penzance 16, 17
Perranzabuloe 39, 56
Picking 6, 31, **33**, 35, 38, 42, 43, 44, 45,
  48, 89, 100-102, 103, 105-106
Poldice 42
Polglaze, Norman **101**, 103
Polgooth 40
Polpuff Glass Mine 93-98
Pregnancy 14, 15, 18-20,
Prouse, Bella 103

Racking 6, 34, 38, 47, 89
Red River Tin Streams 59
Redruth 14, 16, 35, 36
Reinhart, B. S. 77, **78**
Rescorla, Mrs 96
Retallick, Captain Fred 95, 98
Retallick, Gussie 95
Reynolds, Arthur, 103, 104
Rice, Mona 96
Richards, Minnie 86-91, **88**
Richards, Hilda 96
Rickard, Mrs 75-76
Riddling see *sieving*
Rideing, William 77-79
Roberts, William 53

Other publications from the same author

Bal Maidens by Lynne Mayers

Award winning book on the work and lives of the women and girls who worked at the mines, clay pits and slate quarries of Devon and Cornwall. Second & enlarged edition, published by Blaize Bailey Books, 2008. 300 pages, 175mm x 250mm paperback with 81 illustrations, mine and bal maidens indexes.

Available from www.lulu.com

A Dangerous Place to Work! by Lynne Mayers

This book tells the story of the employment of women and children right across the mining industries of Devon and Cornwall, up until the second half of the 20th century. It includes their work at the mines, clay works, slate quarries, foundries, smelters, as well as gunpowder and explosives works. Published by Blaize Bailey Books, 2007. 103 pages, 155mm x 230mm paperback with 20 illustrations.

Available from www.lulu.com